LIFE IN THE RING

LIFE IN THE RING

John E. Oden

Foreword by Bert Randolph Sugar

Illustrated by Brooke L. Adams

Hatherleigh Press is committed to preserving and protecting the natural resources of the Earth. Environmentally responsible and sustainable practices are embraced within the company's mission statement.

Hatherleigh Press is a member of the Publishers Earth Alliance, committed to preserving and protecting the natural resources of the planet while developing a sustainable business model for the book publishing industry.

www.hatherleighpress.com

Library of Congress Cataloging-in-Publication Data

Oden, John E
Life in the ring : lessons and inspiration from the sport of boxing / John Oden.
p. cm.
Includes bibliographical references and index.
ISBN 978-1-57826-311-0 (pbk : alk. paper)
1. Boxing—Anecdotes. I. Title.
GV1135.O46 2009
796.83—dc22
2009029720

All Hatherleigh Press titles are available for bulk purchase, special promotions, and premiums. For information on reselling and special purchase opportunities, call 1-800 528-2550 and ask for the Special Sales Manager.

Interior design by DC Designs
Cover design by Sarah Stern

10 9 8 7 6 5 4 3 2 1
Printed in the United States

For all those friends, acquaintances, and skeptics
who have asked me so many times over the years,
"Why do you like boxing?"

I have never thought of it (boxing) as a sport. There is nothing fundamentally playful about it; nothing that seems to belong to daylight, to pleasure. At its moments of greatest intensity it seems to contain so complete and so powerful an image of life—life's beauty, vulnerability, despair, incalculable and often self-destructive courage—that boxing is life, and hardly a mere game.[1]

—Joyce Carol Oates, *On Boxing*

Contents

Foreword
by Bert Randolph Sugar

Going back almost to the time when Cain rendered Abel *hors de combat,* writers have worn their pencils down to stubs churning out a sumptuous variety of articles and books about the sport of boxing. Some of those in the writing dodge remain as unknown as Whistler's father, but many are as well known as the face that greets us every morning in the bathroom mirror—and include such great writers as Homer, Hazlitt, and Hemingway.

Everyone, it seems has a book in them. So it came as no surprise when a friend of mine named John Oden, a successful businessman and white collar boxer himself, approached me to tell me of his plan to write a book on boxing and asked for my opinion. Now, I've been held up for my opinion with a loaded drink pointed at my head twenty times or more—enough times for all the products of Scotland to be exhausted—but I will admit that, at first, words failed me. All I could do was roll my eyes in their parent sockets and try to dissuade him by telling him about the hardships of writing, how it had been described as everything from an act of courage to a vocation of unhappiness, even throwing in Red Smith's immortal line, "There is nothing to writing. All you do is sit down at a typewriter and open a vein." In short, writing is hardly a barrel of monkeys. I advised John it'd be best to stay away.

Nevertheless, he persevered, desiring only what he could accomplish. And, writing from the smithy of his soul, he accomplished much in producing the book, *White Collar Boxing—One Man's Journey from the Office to the Ring.* Honesty dictates that I tell you it was good: not great, mind you, but good. A different view from a different pew is refreshing, and Oden had told a straightforward story of how he had, as a round peg in the square ring known as boxing, fit. I thought to myself: *Welcome, John, to the amateur division of boxing writing.*

Jump-skip four years later, and John, still with printer's ink in his blood, came back with yet another book idea. This time 'round he wanted to write a book of vignettes, illustrating how boxers could provide everyone, from businessmen on Wall Street to ordinary men on Main Street, with lessons and inspiration. Simple yet impactful messages, to be sure, but ones that could be learned and applied to life.

Studying the sport and its participants the way a scientist would a specimen, Oden chose 15 boxers from almost every era of the sport—from yesteryear's Jack Dempsey and Gene Tunney, to today's Oscar De La Hoya, Bernard Hopkins, and Joe Calzaghe. And, in telling their stories in vivid vignettes and applying the principles learned from them, Oden builds a fascinating, case-by-case study with plainspoken straightforwardness that provides lessons for life.

This is a welcome relief from the many books on boxing that strain to tell us the sordid side of boxing, the scandals that pockmark the face of the sport, and are chronicled with numbing predictability. Oden's is a positive book on the "Sweet Science," which only gets sweeter with its upbeat and inspirational message.

And while some may say an inspirational book on boxing is as unbelievable as Santa Claus suffering from vertigo or Captain Bligh with sea sickness, John Oden has done it, rubbing his creative lamp to give us a book that illuminates the sport in a way different than anyone has before.

John, welcome to the big leagues of boxing writing!

—Bert Randolph Sugar, *July 29, 2009*

Introduction

I HAVE ALWAYS BELIEVED that boxing is a metaphor for life.

In this book you will discover the stories of 15 extraordinary men from all walks of life, from different times and different backgrounds. These men chose boxing as their vocation. Each one brought his own unique contribution to the sport. Their stories are profound and each no two are alike.

You will read of their hardship, struggle, defeat, comeback, and victory. They capture the very essence of the human experience. When a truly competitive boxing match is performed by skilled fighters, there is also a beauty, grace, and athletic excellence which cannot be duplicated in any other sport. And it is that combination of elements which grabs the imagination.

In boxing there are no words, only actions. And behind the action in a boxing ring are many of the human emotions and complications that one might encounter in life—preparation, concentration, purposefulness, goal setting, challenges, pain, perseverance, and a host of anxieties and fears.

There is an aloneness to boxing that is unique in sports. Indeed, when facing an opponent one-on-one, there is only you . . . and him. All the training, all the experience, all the emotions, come with you out of the corner. But there is no team, no ball, no bat, no racquet, no protective shoulder pads for someone to hide behind. And like a gladiatorial contest, it is done until one of the participants or the other cannot go on, either by knockout or stoppage, or when the winner or loser is declared by the judges at the end of the fight.

At its core, boxing is a sport of self-actualization, a means to discover truths about oneself which could not be learned in any other place quite so effectively. In boxing, mental agility and toughness are as equally important as physical strength and ability. Bruce Silverglade, owner of the famous Gleason's Gym in New York City and the "godfather of white collar boxing" maintains that "the only person who can make a champ is the person himself . . . not the trainer, the manager, or anyone else. Boxing is 50 percent mental, 40 percent conditioning, and 10 percent ability." The keys to the sport are commitment and focus. And these come with pain, long hours of preparation, and continued sacrifice. And then comes the day of judgment, the moment of truth—either a boxer wins or loses when he or she climbs between the ropes.

Boxing is ingrained in our culture, and evidence to this effect is everywhere: references to boxing constantly pop up in the lives we lead, and people make analogies to boxing without even realizing it. Nomenclature like "knockout punch," "came out swinging," "took some hard shots," "down for the count," and "main event," are all references to elements of boxing in the society in which we live that make the parallels between life and boxing clear.

In the words of Joyce Carol Oates, "Life is real and painful, and steeped in ambiguity: in the boxing ring there is either/

or. Either you win or you lose."[1] "Boxing's dark fascination is as much with failure, and the courage to forbear failure, as it is with triumph. Two men climb into a ring from which, in symbolic terms, only one climbs out."[2] Indeed, how we handle losing, or winning, can define us in life.

And the last words of caution spoken by the referee to the boxers before the fight begins "protect yourself at all times," is a symbolic caution of what must be done to survive not only in the ring, but in life on a daily basis. From the working world to our own personal lives, one thing is certain: there will come a time when we will have to enter the ring, alone, and face our moment. We can choose to bring heart, character and determination. We can decide to accept that the only result will be victory. And we can triumph.

The poem by Paul Simon, *The Boxer*, contains these lines:

In the clearing stands a boxer
And a fighter by his trade
And he carries the reminders
Of ev'ry glove that laid him down
Or cut him til he cried out
In his anger and his shame
"I am leaving, I am leaving"
But the fighter still remains[3]

Such is life in the ring.

—John E. Oden, *New York City, 2009*

LIFE IN THE RING

MUHAMMAD ALI

Born: January 17, 1942, Louisville, Kentucky

Won WBA and WBC Heavyweight Titles: February 25, 1964 (defeated Sonny Liston)

Forced Inactivity: March 23, 1967 to October 26, 1970

Won WBA and WBC Heavyweight Titles: October 30, 1974 (defeated George Foreman)

Lost WBA and WBC Heavyweight Titles: February 15, 1978 (Leon Spinks)

Won WBA and WBC Heavyweight Titles: September 15, 1978 (defeated Leon Spinks)

Retired 1979, Attempted Comeback in 1980 Failed, Last Fight: 1981

Record: 56 wins, 5 losses, 37 knockouts

Boxing Handle: The Greatest

ROUND ONE

Courage and Confidence

✦ Muhammad Ali ✦

> Ali . . . was a true warrior. It was unbelievable, the courage he had. He wasn't just a championship athlete . . . He was above sports; he was part of history. The man used his athletic ability as a platform to project himself right up there with world leaders, taking chances that absolutely no one else took, going after things that very few people have the courage to go after.[1]
>
> Jim Brown, Hall of Fame football great

For a boxer, courage can make all the difference between success and failure. It takes courage to climb through the ropes of a boxing ring to face an opponent. There, alone and with little to protect him, a boxer faces an opponent whose intended purpose is to stop him in his tracks and put him down.

Muhammad Ali is perhaps the best known athlete of the Twentieth Century. A "character of our time," he electrified crowds with his ability as a boxer, garnering the attention of the world by the force of his personality and attention-grabbing antics. Proclaiming himself "The Greatest," he taunted his opponents long before they got into the ring with him.

Inside the ring, Ali fought them all—all the challengers and champions of his era, ducking no one. Outside the ring, he stood up to anyone who he thought was wrongfully in his way, and fought back with everything he had at social injustices and unfair prejudices. These achievements were fueled by the steadfast courage and unshakeable confidence he displayed to the world.

✦ ✦ ✦

THE MAN KNOWN throughout the world today as Muhammad Ali was born Cassius Marcellus Clay on January 17, 1942 in Louisville, Kentucky. Cassius' father, Cassius Clay, Sr., was a sign painter and an artist. Cassius' mother, Odessa, worked mostly as a housewife and mother, occasionally taking jobs cooking and cleaning for upper-class whites. Many of Cassius Clay's future opponents—whom he would fight after changing his name to Muhammad Ali in 1964—Sonny Liston, Floyd Patterson, Joe Frazier, and George Foreman, among them, were born poor into large families where the father was either out of work or not around. This was not the case for young Cassius, who was well provided for by parents who cared for him.

Cassius Clay's future as a fighter had its unlikely beginnings one day in October of 1954, when, at the age of 12, he went to a local bazaar with one of his friends. Cassius rode his new bike, a sixty dollar, red and white Schwinn of which he was extremely proud. After parking their bikes, Cassius and his friend wandered around the bazaar, killing time and enjoying free popcorn and ice cream. But when they decided to head home, Cassius discovered that his new Schwinn was gone. He was livid. Cassius sought out a local police officer, Joe Martin, who was manning a basement boxing gym in the neighborhood. Cassius demanded the police search for his bike, and, in a fury, swore he would beat up whoever had stolen from him. Martin, who also did some boxing training and coaching, replied by suggesting that Cassius take some boxing lessons before he challenged anyone to a fight. Soon, Cassius began training at Martin's gym.

From the beginning, it was clear that there were many things that made young Cassius Clay unique. He learned quickly, and showed marked speed and athletic prowess. He was also incredibly disciplined. As a teenager, Clay was fortunate that he did not have to work, and could therefore throw everything he had into his training when he wasn't in school. When Clay wasn't running in the early morning hours as he did daily, he all but lived at the gym, working out after school and on into the evening. A far cry from your typical teen, he never drank, never smoked, and only ate healthfully in an effort to keep his body "pure." A polite, respectful young man, he never used his fisticuff talents outside the gym. He was shy around girls and was often seen reading the Bible that he often carried with him. Clay's exemplary behavior and fine manners were largely the result of his mother's positive influence. But his drive and dedication came from within.

By his mid-teens, Clay had been training as hard as some professional boxers. Once he hit the amateur circuit, he picked up six Kentucky Golden Gloves championships, two National Golden Gloves championships, and finished his amateur career with a record of 100 wins in 108 fights. Clay entered the 1960 Olympic Games in Rome and took home the gold medal in the light heavyweight division at the age of 18.

Months after his Olympic win, Clay turned pro. He soon

developed a ring technique which was driven by his personal confidence. His trademarks became his headhunting style, never throwing body punches, as he could use his reach to deliver solid blows, but could dance away before an opponent could get close enough to hit him. His feet were so fast that he seemed to float in the ring, and to delight the crowd he would occasionally shuffle them rapidly in a blazing motion that eventually became known as the "Ali Shuffle." He would sometimes fight with his hands lowered, almost as if inviting his adversary to try to hit him—if someone came forward, he would either dance out of harm's way or make his opponent pay by unleashing a barrage of rapid punches that would make his adversary think twice before trying the move again.

There were other changes in his approach to the sport and the demeanor he displayed to the public, likely the result of his exposure to international competition from his Olympic days and his continuing evolution as a thinking athlete and a man. He began to recite poetry to describe his ring encounters and boxing experiences. He would do this before each fight, actually predicting the round that he would stop his opponent. Also, over time, his quiet demeanor was replaced by a brash, attention-getting, outspoken personal style which captured the public's imagination. All of these came together to portray him as a confident boxer with the courage to carry off his unorthodox fighting methods. With this array of boxing skills and headline-grabbing appeal to boxing fans, he was able to connect all the dots to produce a winning combination—he kept winning and the crowds loved him.

One of the first major tests of Clay's true confidence and courage came in 1964 at the age of 22, when he got a shot at the World Heavyweight Championship against the reigning champion, Sonny Liston. By then, Clay had an impressive record of 19-0, including 15 knockouts. Liston's record was 35-1, with 25 knockouts, including two recent first round knockouts over former Heavyweight Champion Floyd Patterson, from whom he had taken the title. Liston was considered unbeatable by many, an opponent who could never be fazed. As fearsome a ring general as boxing had ever known, Liston's powerful arms threw bomb after unforgiving bomb. Unlike Clay, Liston had a difficult childhood that bred violence: beaten throughout his childhood by his brutal father, an Arkansas cotton picker, Liston was convicted of armed robbery at an early age, and learned to box in prison. Powerful and menacing in the ring, Liston could have been cast by Hollywood in his role as Heavyweight Champion. His sole loss prior to his fight with Clay was to a journeyman opponent named Marty Marshall in 1954, when Marshall managed to break Liston's jaw with a right hand while Liston was laughing at him. Liston's ferocious punching power was matched only by his threatening scowl and intimidating personality. Many considered it too soon in Clay's career for him to attempt to take on Liston.

Although the odds-makers favored Liston by 7-1, Clay was confident he would find a way to win. At the press conference with Liston, on February 25, 1964, Clay devised an interesting approach—he seemingly went crazy. He came into the Miami Beach Auditorium waving a big stick and screaming insults at

Liston, calling him a "big ugly bear." Clay was fined by local boxing officials for misconduct and observers questioned whether Clay was physically or mentally capable of fighting, as his heart was pounding and his blood pressure extremely high. For his part, Liston didn't know exactly what he was up against, although he guessed that Clay was either crazy or terrified. Of course, an hour later in his dressing room, Clay was fine, blood pressure and heart rate both normal, and these antics were merely part of Clay's attempts to psych out Liston.

Clay took control of the fight from the opening bell, and Liston had trouble hitting him. Liston, who was known to lift people off the ground with his jab, couldn't even touch Clay. Clay's footwork simply kept him out of reach, and Liston kept throwing big punches, most of them missing badly. Clay was able to land some nice punches on Liston, gaining respect as the fight went on, and by the third round, Liston had a cut under his left eye. Clay's plan was to keep moving, tire him out, and then go on the attack. Clay was in complete control.

In the corner between rounds four and five, Clay complained that he had something in his eyes which burned them and he could not see. The pain was excruciating, and Clay screamed at Angelo Dundee, his corner man, who rinsed his eyes with a sponge and told him to go out and stay away from Liston. It is theorized that a medication or liniment used for Liston's cuts and injuries may have gotten in Clay's eyes, but this has never been confirmed. Somehow surviving the fifth by a combination of tying up and "yard-sticking" Liston, as Dundee had instructed Clay (keeping Liston away by stiff arm-ing him, thereby keeping his distance from Liston), Clay took some punishment but managed to survive, with his eyes clearing up towards the end of the round. Liston had won the round, but the rest of the fight was all Clay. Liston did not answer the bell for the seventh round, complaining of a shoulder injury. Cassius Clay became the newly crowned Heavyweight Champion of the World. The odds makers and the public at large were in disbelief—not only had Clay beaten the odds at 7-1, but he had the courage to fight practically blind for most of a round against one of the most intimidating boxers in heavyweight history and managed to survive and win.

A few days later, on March 6, 1964, he was given the name Muhammad Ali by the Honorable Elijah Muhammad, the founder of the Nation of Islam, and became a practicing Muslim minister. He continued to box, defending his title several times in the next 2-3 years, including a first round knockout victory in a rematch against Liston in 1965, and victories over Floyd Patterson in 1965, and Zora Folley in 1967, among others.

Meanwhile, outside the boxing ring, the Vietnam War was tearing the country apart, and, like many young men at the time, Ali would soon be forced to weigh his own personal convictions and decide if the war was one he believed in enough to fight. Ali decided this was not the case: on April 28, 1967, at the age of 25, he formally refused to be inducted into the U.S. Army on the grounds of his religious beliefs. A national furor erupted, with some praising Ali for risking prison to stand up for his beliefs, and others calling him a draft dodger and a traitor. When asked to explain his actions, Ali said, "I ain't got no quarrel with them Viet Cong. . . . They never called me nigger."[2,3]

Ali's words were emblematic of an era fraught with racial conflict, and, as years passed, his statement was regarded as one that characterized the era itself. For Ali, this type of declarative statement—deceiving in its simplicity, deep in its meaning—would come to define his public persona. But his act of courage had consequences. After refusing to be inducted into the army, the World Boxing Association stripped him of his title and, along with every state and local entity in America, cancelled his licenses and banned him from fighting in the U.S. Furthermore, after being charged with violating the Selective Service Act, Ali's passport was taken, and he was sentenced to 5 years in prison.

Although Ali ended up serving only a brief portion of his prison term, his boxing career suffered. With no license to fight, Ali was out of the ring for 3½ years. During this time, he was able to make money by speaking out against the war. Ali's ability to stand up for his beliefs and stick by his convictions took tremendous courage and confidence during this highly charged moment in U.S. history.

Finally the Supreme Court reversed his conviction and Ali was able to return to the ring in 1970. By this time, he was nearly 29, and he had sacrificed some of his absolute prime boxing years for the principles in which he believed. It is not an overstatement that Ali's refusal to be inducted into the army was one of the most courageous acts in the history of sports.

Over the next four years, Ali fought frequently, including seesaw matches with Joe Frazier and Ken Norton, where he exchanged victories with both fighters. The match with Frazier on March 8, 1971, was labeled "The Fight of the Century" since it marked Ali's attempt to regain the Heavyweight Championship against Frazier, and both fighters were undefeated at the time. Ali was unsuccessful in this first bout against Frazier, but other fighters were defeated in his wake, including Jerry Quarry (two victories in 1970 and 1972), Jimmy Ellis in 1971, George Chuvalo (for the second time in 1972), Floyd Patterson (for the second time in 1972), and Joe Bugner in 1973.

In 1974, four years after returning to the ring, Ali would once again have to call upon his resources of courage and confidence in a bout with World Heavyweight Champion George Foreman. At that point in their careers, Foreman had an incredibly impressive record of 40-0, with 37 knockouts, and Ali weighed in with a record of 44-2, with 29 knockouts. However, Foreman was often compared to Sonny Liston in terms of his glowering personality and ring presence, and was considered by many to be flat-out unbeatable. Foreman was a hulking, threatening, giant of a man who was as powerful as he was big, and frequently knocked out his opponents in a crushing fashion. Additionally, Foreman had destroyed two fighters who had beaten Ali, Joe Frazier and Ken Norton, knocking both men out in the second round.

Everyone in Ali's camp was painfully aware of the 3-1 betting line favoring Foreman. But there was also an unspoken, very real fear that Ali was in for a horrible beating circulating through the camp, a fear based on fact: during his fight with Joe Frazier in 1973, Foreman unleashed a huge uppercut that actually lifted Frazier off the floor. Frazier was knocked down a total of six times before the referee mercifully called a halt to the action.

During the weeks leading up to the fight, scheduled for October 30, 1974, in Kinshasa, Zaire, Ali was his characteristically charismatic self, mingling with the citizens of Kinshasa and leading them in the chant "Ali boom-aye-yay," which in Swahili means "Ali, kill him." In contrast, Foreman was rarely seen in public, and, true to form, was stone-faced and scowling during any appearance.

When it came to training regimens, George was convinced that Ali was scared of him and that their match up would be short and, for Foreman, sweet. Thanks to the knockouts Foreman served up early on in recent fights, he had not had to endure more than four rounds in one single fight in over three years. Foreman had no reason to expect that his bout with Ali would be any different. So Foreman spent most of his training time relaxing in his luxurious air-conditioned Hilton penthouse suite. Ali, by contrast, adopted a serious training regimen. As the 3-1 underdog, Ali knew full well the challenge which lay ahead of him, and that he would have be in his best physical condition. His training was specifically designed to help him adapt to the intense African heat. In addition to running to the point of exhaustion, his training consisted of 19 rounds per day, nine of which consisted of sparring with three partners.

After a delay of several weeks due to an injury Foreman suffered in a sparring session, the "Rumble in the Jungle," finally took place the day before Halloween, on October 30, 1974, with storm clouds lingering above the open-air ring. Ali came out of his dressing room first, walking to the ring methodically and confidently in his white robe. A short time later Foreman jogged to the ring in his red robe, entering in his menacing fashion and looking the part of the anvil-fisted, giant-killer that he was. While the referee was giving his customary instructions to the fighters in the center of the ring, Ali began to talk to Foreman, while Foreman just stood there staring him down in a glaringly fierce manner.

Ali started strong in the first round, and stood his ground against the monstrous Foreman. Foreman had expected Ali to run away, but Ali was aggressive from the opening bell, trading blow-for-blow with Foreman. During the first round, Ali surprised Foreman (and probably himself) by throwing a dozen right hand leads. This type of punch requires great confidence for a right handed fighter, as it has to cross the additional distance across the shoulders before the fighter delivering the punch can recover his stance. Ali pulled it off, with several of his shots connecting and rattling Foreman.

Then, in a further show of confidence beginning in the second round, Ali set up his "rope-a-dope" strategy, where he retreated to the ropes, blocking punches while Foreman hammered away with big, wild, roundhouse punches, tiring himself out. Many at ringside at first thought that Ali was being overwhelmed by Foreman. However, Foreman did little serious damage to Ali, who, effectively blocked and covered himself, and also preserved energy in the process. All the while, Ali taunted Foreman, goading him on by saying, "Is that the best you got? Is that the hardest you can hit, chump? Show me sumthing, George. That don't hurt, that's a sissy punch!"[4]

For the remainder of the fight, Ali let Foreman swing away for much of the round, and then, when Foreman least expected it, Ali would rally with a flurry of punches as the round ended. Weakened by the effects of the muggy monsoon season in Zaire and his own lack of stamina, Foreman lumbered around the ring and appeared so weak that it seemed as if he had to push every punch, and was sagging visibly. Ali fought defensively, expertly and accurately, blocking shots and conserving energy. Towards the end of the eighth round, Ali moved off the ropes and mounted a spectacular attack. He knocked Foreman down and out, and, with that, reclaimed his WBA and WBC Heavyweight Titles in what history has labeled one of the most exciting and dramatic heavyweight fights ever. It can be said that this was his finest hour as a boxer: Ali showed the entire world that his courage and resolve could overcome odds overwhelmingly stacked against him.

For the next seven years, Ali continued to fight, sometimes impressively, sometimes not. He won his third match in 1975 against Joe Frazier in the Philippines, a third one against Ken Norton in 1976, won a decision against Ernie Shavers in 1977, and traded victories with Leon Spinks in 1978 (losing the WBA and WBC Heavyweight Titles and then reclaiming them for a third time). He announced his retirement in

1979, but attempted a comeback when he challenged former sparring partner, Larry Holmes, for the Heavyweight Title one last time in 1980, resulting in a disappointing TKO stoppage. His final match was a loss against Trevor Berbick on December 11, 1981, a few days shy of his 40th birthday.

But Ali was to face an even greater battle than any he had faced in the ring. As Muhammad Ali's boxing career started to wind down in the late 70's, he began to show decreasing motor skills and signs of neurological disorder. After seeing several doctors in 1984, Ali was officially diagnosed with Parkinson's, a debilitating, degenerative disease of the central nervous system that often impairs motor skills, speech and other functions, and is characterized by muscle rigidity, tremors and slowing of physical movement. Although Parkinson's is not a disease confined to those who have spent their careers in the boxing ring, Ali's case was noted to have been likely brought on by repetitive head trauma from his career as a boxer.

Yet even in his compromised physical state, Ali's courage and confidence remained strong, even when he was called to the spotlight. On the opening night of the Olympic Games in July of 1996 in Atlanta, Georgia, eighty-five thousand people from all over the world gathered in the stands for the opening ceremonies. Additionally, three and one-half million people watched on television worldwide. Preparations for this night had been underway for years and the secret of who would light the torch was very closely guarded—almost no one in the stadium knew who would have those special honors.

Whoever was to light the Olympic Flame would be handed

the Olympic Torch after it had passed through a series of hands. First, four-time Olympic gold medalist and discuss thrower American Al Oerter entered the stadium with the torch held high and handed it to Olympic bronze medalist and professional boxing champion Evander Holyfield. The excitement of the crowd was building as the moment to light the torch grew near. Greek hurdler and Olympic gold medalist Voula Patoulidou joined Holyfield and they passed the torch to Olympic gold medalist and swimmer, Janet Evans. The enthusiasm of the crowd continued to build. The crowd rose to their feet as Janet Evans started up the long ramp leading to the Olympic Cauldron, the source of the flame that would burn every day of the Olympic Games.

Then, out of the shadows at the top of the ramp appeared a single figure, a man in white. He stood tall and straight and held the receiving torch with both hands. It was Muhammad Ali. The crowd gasped in astonishment and joy.

After Janet Evans lit Ali's torch, he lifted it high with both arms. Then, without a moment's pause or uncertainty, he let down his left arm, and held the torch with only his right arm, for all to see. His left arm quivered uncontrollably, but Ali, undaunted, held the torch high with his right hand as he looked out over the crowd. He then bent down to light the fuse that would transport the flame to the cauldron high above the stadium. With the Olympic Cauldron lit, Ali stood to face the crowd and the stadium exploded with cheers. Muhammad Ali stood proud at the top of the stadium before the eyes of the world.

When he had been asked to light the Olympic Flame, Ali accepted the challenge without hesitation. His reduced motor skills did not stop him, and he did not back down from the responsibility of facing a worldwide audience of millions. It can be said that this one moment captured the unfettered image of Ali's Olympic youth, and summarized the enduring spirit and courage of the man.

Muhammad Ali lives in a world that he created for himself, one defined by his ingenuity, talent and determination, and, above all, his courage and confidence in the unrelenting pursuit of his goals. Challenging anything that stood in his way, this hallmark of American originality imposed his one-of-a-kind personality, style and creativity on the world, changing it as he went along, and enjoying every moment. As a confirmation to the influence he had on sports and the world, and the courage he had demonstrated to all as he had made his unparalleled journey, he was named "Sportsman of the Century" in 1999 by *Sports Illustrated.*

Since he retired from boxing, Muhammad Ali has devoted himself to humanitarian endeavors in the United States and around the globe, as he travels the world lending his name and presence to hunger and poverty relief, supporting educational efforts of all kinds. Championing the issues in the developing world has also become a major focus of his life, and it is estimated that he has been instrumental in providing more than 232 million meals to feed the world's hungry. In 2005, he received the Presidential Medal of Freedom, the United States of America's highest civil award.

✦ ✦ ✦

Inside and outside the ring, Ali displayed incredible courage and confidence. To the world, his accomplishments as a boxer were remarkable, but so was his steadfast resolve to defend the principles in which he believed.

In anything in life, acting with confidence and courage in the face of a great challenge can make the difference between winning and losing, despite the odds that may be stacked against you. For Ali, the image which he presented to the public was his "magic," and revealed to the world a man who had the courage of a lion and unshakable confidence. In life, combining confidence with the courage to act is a winning formula for success in almost any endeavor. Being able to back up these traits with skill and ability, and the determination to win and succeed, combined with his unwavering commitment to the principles in which he believed, propelled Muhammad Ali to legendary status, not only in the sport of boxing, but to the entire world.

Fortune favors the bold.

—Virgil, Roman poet

JACK DEMPSEY

Born: June 24, 1895, Manassa, Colorado.
Died: May 31, 1983, New York City
Won World Heavyweight Title: July 4, 1919 (defeated Jess Willard)
Lost World Heavyweight Title: September 23, 1926 (Gene Tunney)
Record: 61 wins, 6 losses, 8 draws, 6 no-decisions, 50 knockouts
Boxing Handle: The Manassa Mauler

GENE TUNNEY

Born: May 25, 1897, New York City.
Died: November 7, 1978, Greenwich, Connecticut
Won American Light Heavyweight Title: January 13, 1922 (defeated Battling Levinsky)
Lost American Light Heavyweight Title: May 23, 1922 (Harry Greb)
Regained American Light Heavyweight Title: February 23, 1923 (defeated Harry Greb)
Won World Heavyweight Title: September 23, 1926 (defeated Jack Dempsey)
Retired as World Heavyweight Champion: July 31, 1928
Record: 61 wins, 1 loss, 1 draw, 1 no-contest, 19 no-decisions, 45 knockouts
Boxing Handle: The Fighting Marine

ROUND TWO

Great Opponents Make Great Champions

✦ Jack Dempsey and Gene Tunney ✦

There is nothing like a challenge to bring out the best in man.

—Sean Connery, Actor

The matches between Gene Tunney and Jack Dempsey were two of the best the sport has ever produced. It pitted two of the best heavyweight boxers of that, or any, era, against one another. They fought two epic battles in 1926 and 1927 which defined both of their careers—and their lives—and they will forever be remembered for these bouts. Their two encounters demonstrate how great the sport can be when two talented boxers can square off against each other and help each other rise to the occasion and give performances far beyond what would ordinarily be expected.

In boxing, if a great boxer is not challenged, he is not able to showcase his skills. A strong opponent imposes risks and uncertainties into any competitive situation, which, if harnessed properly, can help someone reach a higher level they are trying to achieve, bypassing what they might ordinarily expect of themselves. For Dempsey and Tunney, it was in fighting each other that they pushed their individual performances to another level, and helped one another be the best they could be.

✦ ✦ ✦

In 1920, a handsome ex-Marine riding the Hudson River ferry from Jersey City to Manhattan met World Heavyweight Boxing Champion Jack Dempsey. The two men chatted for a while and, although the Marine liked and admired Dempsey, the Marine was also a boxer, and, with that fighter's instinct and drive to win, could not help himself from calculating ways he could beat Dempsey someday. As time went by, the Marine continued to obsess about how to beat Dempsey and take the title for himself. The Marine was Gene Tunney, and years later, he would get his wish and face the champion in the ring in two of the most memorable fights ever.

In many ways Jack Dempsey and Gene Tunney were similar; both were determined, skilled fighters from humble backgrounds who overcame challenges to gain success in the ring, and later in life. In other ways, though, they were as different as night and day—it was a classic match-up of a tough-guy slugger/puncher in Dempsey, against a disciplined and skilled ring artisan in Tunney.

In other words, you couldn't have dreamed up a better rivalry.

JACK DEMPSEY

Stated simply, Jack Dempsey was larger than life. Named after U.S. President William Harrison, William Harrison Dempsey (later "Jack") grew up in the small town of Manassa in the flatlands of Southern Colorado. Dempsey was one of eleven children born to Mormon farmers, Hyrum and Celia Smoot Dempsey, who had a combined lineage with elements of Scottish, Irish, Cherokee and Choctaw. Celia Dempsey was a tiny woman, weighing about 100 pounds. She was a staunch Mormon; Hyrum took more readily to alcohol and tobacco. In order to keep the family afloat, Hyrum worked to put food on the table at whatever came along, including teaching and shoveling ore in the mines. Still, the family fell on hard times, and young Dempsey dropped out of grade school to work, washing dishes at the age of 11.

Over the years, young Dempsey took whatever job he could find, including picking crops, working as a saloon bouncer, pitching hay, shining shoes, and herding cattle. At 16, he left home. For the next few years, Dempsey lived as hobo, riding the rails from town to town and living in the hobo jungles. With work becoming more and more difficult to obtain, Dempsey began using his newly discovered fighting prowess to earn a few bucks. He would fight anybody, anywhere—he even fought for coins or his supper in small mining towns. During this time, he had countless unrecorded fights in barrooms, saloons, in the open air or in streets of small mining towns. Dempsey took his fights seriously: it was during this period that he began soaking his face and hands in beef brine to harden them before a fight.

From 1914, to 1917, Dempsey pursued a boxing career out West, largely in Colorado, Utah and Nevada. When the United States entered World War One (WW1) in 1917, Dempsey attempted to enlist in the U.S. Army but was turned down, so, instead, he spent the war years working in a shipyard while continuing to box in his free time.

In 1917, Dempsey met Jack Kearns in a San Francisco bar. Kearns, a shrewd ex-fighter turned gambler and small-time manager, had the interesting habit of carrying his cuts equipment in a small black bag and was known as "Doc." Dempsey moved in with Doc, who organized Dempsey's career in a deliberate manner, supervising his training and personal habits, and picking his opponents carefully. Under Doc's tutelage, the 23-year-old Dempsey boxed 21 times in 1918 alone with only one defeat.

Dempsey started out the year 1919 with an attention grabbing record of five victories in a row, all by knockout in the first round. With these successes, Dempsey was getting noticed in the boxing world. Already, his style of boxing was known to strike fear into the hearts of his opponents. Dempsey would stalk his adversary from a crouched position, studying him for any sign of weakness or hesitation, and then, when the time was right, "unleash hell" with a devastating fistic assault. With dark, penetrating eyes, Dempsey had a menacing ring appearance, combined with lightning hand speed, and a take-no-prisoners-ferociousness that the crowds loved. He captured the imagination of a country that still believed in the virtues of toughness and individuality. Little was Dempsey to know that two of his greatest matches would not come until the end of the next decade.

In 1919, after Kearns introduced Dempsey to legendary promoter Tex Rickard, a former horse wrangler, U.S. marshal, saloon owner and gold panner, Dempsey was booked for a world title fight against World Heavyweight Champion Jess Willard, the man who had dethroned Jack Johnson. Over the ensuing years, it was the genius of Rickard—a combination of P.T. Barnum and Don King—that would take full advantage of Dempsey's rough and tumble image. Though Kearns and Rickard weren't exactly the best of friends, their partnership with Dempsey became known as the "Golden Triangle," and Kearns and Rickard would, with Dempsey's success and stardom, make millions.

On Independence Day, July 4, 1919, Dempsey faced down Jess Willard. At 6'6" and 250 pounds, Willard towered 5½ inches over Dempsey, and outweighed him by an incredible 58 pounds. Despite his physical disadvantages, Dempsey, who had caught wind of the rumor that Kearns had bet the challenger's entire purse on a first-round win, came into the ring like a man possessed. Dempsey floored Willard seven times within the first round. Willard did not get off of his stool for the fourth round, and Jack Dempsey was the new World Heavyweight Champion. Evidence of Dempsey's brute strength was written on Willard's face: his cheekbone and jaw were fractured in multiple places, and six of his teeth had been hammered out of his mouth when the final bell rang. Additionally, Willard's left ear was so severely mauled that he never regained proper hearing in it. The damage to Willard was so incredible that it drew speculation over the years that Dempsey's hand wrappings inside his gloves were soaked in plaster of Paris, a charge which Dempsey denied throughout his life.

After winning the title, Jack Dempsey made publicity appearances around the country, at circuses, exhibitions, and other promotional events. Between 1919 and 1923, each time the "Manassa Mauler" successfully defended his title, crowds of thousands would gather and listeners on the radio all around the country (and occasionally in various parts of the world) would tune in. During this time, Dempsey participated in the quickest fight on record of that day (knocked out Carl Morris in 14 seconds) and brought in the first million dollar gate against George Carpentier on July 2, 1921. It seemed like all of Dempsey's fights during this era were sensational for one reason or another. For one, his fights often became an incalculable, all-out, no-holds-barred brawl, where anything and everything could (and did) happen. Fight after fight, Dempsey was establishing himself as an unpredictable force to be reckoned with, notorious for his ring exploits; in other words, Dempsey did not disappoint. Whenever Dempsey stepped into the "squared circle," he grabbed headlines and sold seats like never before in the history of the sport.

Yet a true champion is only as great as the opponents and

challenges he is willing to undertake. On September 14, 1923, Argentinean Luis Firpo, a.k.a. the "Wild Bull of the Pampas," challenged Dempsey before a crowd of almost 90,000 people in New York's Polo Grounds, (with another 20,000 trying to get in; that's nearly twice the seating in the new Yankee Stadium.). In Buenos Aries, it was broadcast over primitive radios and people gathered in the streets to listen in. In the first round, Dempsey put down Firpo an amazing seven times, but, by the end of the round, the Argentinean countered with a surprising overhand right that sent Dempsey out of the ring and onto the press box. Fortunately, Dempsey was pushed back into the ring just in time to avoid being counted out. This moment was later immortalized by the American painter George Bellows in his classic and timeless work *Dempsey and Firpo.* In round two, the "Manassa Mauler" hit back, knocking Firpo down twice, and claiming a victory in one of the wildest fights on record—all of which occurred in less than four minutes.

After the Firpo fight, Dempsey took 3 years off from boxing and even experimented with filmmaking as an actor. One of the movies he acted in was a feature film called *Manhattan Madness,* and during the filming he met a beautiful young actress named Estelle Taylor. Romance blossomed, and the couple was married in 1924. The news media had a field day, snapping photos of the couple wherever they went. One classic pose showed Estelle perched six feet off the ground, on Dempsey's shoulders. Dempsey enjoyed the glamorous high life with his beautiful movie star wife, and enjoying their place as the toasts-of-the-town wherever they went, which included long stays in Estelle's favorite city, Paris. His fans loved Dempsey's brashness in the ring and his glamour outside of it.

From the start of the Prohibition era in 1919 until the 1929 stock market crash, it was Dempsey who captured the imagination of an adoring public. He was a force of nature and the great boxing hero of the Jazz Age, the tumultuous 20's, where he reigned supreme as World Heavyweight Champion for seven years, from 1919 until 1926. It was an era when ordinary men dreamed big, and underdog heroes were welcomed and worshipped. Still, throughout all, Dempsey remained down-to-earth and personable, a man who never forgot his roots and conversed with people of all economic circumstances.

When Dempsey returned to boxing, his greatest test as a champion was waiting in the wings, in the form of a handsome, gentlemanly, articulate, and calculating, ex-Marine, Gene Tunney.

GENE TUNNEY

Gene Tunney was the second of seven children of Irish immigrants, an unassuming boy from a modest working-class family in Greenwich Village in New York City. His mother, Mary Lydon from Kiltimagh, Ireland, immigrated to the United States after the potato famine and settled in New York City, where she met and married John Tunney, also from Kiltimagh. When Gene was 10 years old, his longshoreman father presented him with a pair of boxing gloves. Young Gene took to boxing right away, fighting in the streets and later in the amateur ring. Gene grew into a tall and movie-star handsome man, and, the same month he turned 21, he volunteered for the Marines in WW1. While in the Marines, he boxed for the American Expeditionary Forces and, by war's end, became the armed forces Light Heavyweight Champion.

Upon his return, Tunney wasted no time and set about to pursue a professional boxing career. However, despite his success in the Marines, he got off to a rough start; he simply wasn't in demand with fight managers and promoters, and, further, he could not afford boxing equipment. Luckily, he met Billy Roche, a well-connected manager who on December 19, 1919, was able to arrange an eight round fight for Tunney which he won easily. The next morning he had $150 in earnings, which he proudly showed his mother. (She had always wished her son would become a priest or businessman.)

While Dempsey was basking in the glory of his status as World Heavyweight Champion, and fighting occasionally, Tunney was trudging through the competitive rankings in the light heavyweight division. Known as "The Fighting Marine," Tunney was a gifted ring general, known for his ease, confidence and meticulous control—he was a true student of the "sweet science." Ambitious and focused, Tunney studiously observed each opponent; then he set about, in his methodical manner, to bring him down. He was also viewed by the public as an intellectual outside the ring. In his off hours, he read widely from Shakespeare, and enjoyed the company of the Irish playwright George Bernard Shaw, F. Scott Fitzgerald, and Ernest Hemingway. Because of his cerebral approach to boxing and life, Tunney did not enjoy the same widespread celebrity status as Dempsey. Nevertheless, Tunney had many successful fights that defined him as a boxer and set the stage for his encounter with the rival he had long fantasized about, Jack Dempsey. In short, Gene Tunney just kept winning and winning until Dempsey was forced to take notice.

While Tunney's studious and meticulous nature helped to make him a good boxer, he always attributed his five fights with Harry Greb as the catalysts that turned him from a good boxer into a *great* one. From Greb, Tunney learned how to fight a "no holds barred," "take no prisoners," "break all the rules" fighter, which proved invaluable over the course of his career and eventually helped prepare him for his later fights with Dempsey.

When Greb met Tunney, Greb was past his peak, blind in one eye (although Tunney didn't know this—Greb kept it a secret), four inches shorter and 12 pounds lighter than Tunney. Nevertheless, on May 23, 1922, Greb, "The Human Windmill," dealt Tunney the only loss in his career, and gave him a severe beating using every dirty tactic in the book, including head butting, fouling, holding, and general rough-housing that resulted in a broken nose for Tunney and gashes over both eyes. Tunney simply could not deal with Greb's amazing speed, unorthodox style, and swarming attack. Although he managed to finish the full 15 rounds, Tunney collapsed while leaving the ring, and had to be carried to the dressing room. He spent several days in the hospital recovering. After he healed, Tunney was determined to learn from his mistakes, and devised a plan which would allow him to prevail against an opponent with Greb's ferociousness in the ring and hyperactivity.

Tunney had faced a powerful competitive force in Greb and he knew he would have to change his approach if he was going to beat someone possibly even greater than Greb—namely, Jack Dempsey. In his careful, studious approach to the sport for which he was known, Tunney carefully analyzed Greb in the ensuing nine months, and revised his technique with the help of ring strategist and friend, World Lightweight Champion Benny Leonard. Leonard showed Tunney how to dismantle Greb with artful body punches under the heart, which would take the steam out of Greb. Tunney's work paid off, and he later handed Greb four successive defeats, leaving Greb with two broken ribs in their last encounter for good measure. Now, Tunney felt ready to take on Dempsey.

THE LEGENDARY FIGHTS

The Roaring Twenties was a great time to be an American. It was a generally affluent time, and the increasing affordability and availability of the automobile brought the country closer together as, for the first time, long-distance recreational travel was possible for the average American. In turn, more people were attending sports events across the nation, of which world championship boxing matches drew some of the largest crowds. The drama and intensity of the sport, combined with the allure of fame and fortune, made boxing practically irresistible to crowds. Once more, for the sons of many immigrants, boxing presented a chance at a better life, and most towns had local boxing clubs. Consequently, boxing exploded as one of the most popular sports of the time. This scenario provided a perfect backdrop for the two match-ups between Dempsey and Tunney.

Although Dempsey and Tunney were equally powerful in the ring, their boxing styles were in direct contrast to each other—while Tunney was smooth and controlled, Dempsey was roguish and threatening. Dempsey was a brawling slugger/puncher; Tunney a methodical and calculating ring strategist. Their two fights in 1926 and 1927 are regarded as boxing classics in which two polarized styles collided. The result was a clash of titans in which each man brought nothing short of the best he had to offer into the ring.

Since that fateful meeting on the ferry crossing the Hudson in 1920, Tunney had pondered methodically at analyzing Dempsey's moves in the ring. He had no doubt he would prevail over Dempsey—and he didn't hesitate to share his analysis with the world. "I've seen Dempsey fight and I was impressed by his lack of knowledge of boxing," he said. "He is a great natural fighter but I'm certain that I can outbox him . . . I know I'm a faster and straighter hitter than Dempsey."[1] Tunney added, with the characteristic confidence and certainty of someone accustomed to making intellectual assessments: "Jack never was much of a stayer. By that I mean he fights so fast in the early part of the bout that he tires quickly."[2]

When their first match was finally arranged, both men were at the end of their careers, with remarkably similar records.

Dempsey's record stood at 60 wins (50 KOs), four losses, eight draws, and six no-decisions. Tunney sported a record of 58 wins (44 KOs), one loss, one draw, one no-contest, 19 no--decisions. It was a classic match-up.

Their first meeting was in Philadelphia on September 23, 1926, to a packed house of over 120,000 fans. Collectively, the crowd had paid just shy of $1.9 million to witness Tunney challenge Dempsey's World Heavyweight Title. Due to Dempsey's prolonged time away from the ring, coupled with being two years Tunney's senior, Dempsey had insisted on a 10 round fight, instead of the standard 15 for a title fight. Upon hearing this request, Tunney's confidence increased tenfold, as he surmised that Dempsey questioned his own endurance. With this knowledge in hand, Tunney planned to move around the ring and stay as far away from Dempsey as possible during the contest in an effort to wear him down.

For Dempsey, this first fight with Tunney was less of an epic, topsy-turvy, barn-burner event in comparison to his previous bouts with Willard and Firpo. Although Dempsey stalked Tunney continually, Tunney piled up points by moving away while throwing sharp jabs to Dempsey's face. Tunney used his knowledge of Dempsey's ring-movement well, and managed to stay away from the huffing, puffing Dempsey for the entire 10 rounds. Tunney was awarded the decision. Yet Dempsey left the ring to a tidal wave of cheers, not boos. Somehow, his image was elevated despite his loss. Already, Tex Rickard was licking his chops at the prospect of a rematch that would be sure to shatter all box-office records—the public couldn't get enough. Indeed, the next day, the story occupied a three tier banner headline on the front page of *The New York Times*, along with a two column photograph of new World Heavyweight Champion Gene Tunney. There were 25 stories relating to the fight, including six on the front page alone.

Exactly 364 days later, the time had come for the second meeting between the two ring giants. September 22, 1927, was a hot night in Chicago, where a crowd of over 100,000 fans packed into Soldier Field to see if Jack Dempsey would exact his revenge and regain the title that many felt was rightfully his. Rickard had worked his magic once again, and ticket sales at the gate produced an incredible $2,658,000—a record that would remain untouched for over a half a century, until Muhammad Ali boxed Leon Spinks in 1978. (This phenomenal turnout made Tunney the first boxer in the history of the sport to receive $1 million in a single contest. Actually he received a purse of $990,445 and wrote his own check to Rickard for the difference so that he accepted a check of a round $1 million.) Dempsey earned about half that. While odds makers had the betting favoring Tunney 7-5, the crowd's cheers made it obvious that they were behind Dempsey from the start.

During the first few rounds, many in the crowd must have had déjà vu; like their match in '26, the first six rounds saw Tunney evading Dempsey and piling up points. By round six, he was ahead on all judges' cards. But the fight took a dramatic turn in the early part of the seventh round, when Dempsey unleashed a right hand to Tunney's jaw, which rocked the ex-Marine to the ropes. Spotting a prime opportunity, Dempsey went in for the kill, dealing a heavy left hook and a flurry of punches that put Tunney down on the canvas. The crowd erupted—this was the only time anyone had ever brought the Irishman to the floor. But then, seconds later, confusion erupted. Rather than going to a neutral corner so the referee could commence the count—per a recent addition to the rule book—Dempsey stood hovering over Tunney, losing precious seconds before the referee could commence the count.

Some historians estimate that as many as 14-17 seconds had actually lapsed before the referee reached his normal count of 9—seconds that, in the opinion of many, Dempsey could have used to finish off Tunney, who might have been too dazed to hit back. But rules were rules, and Tunney took advantage of the situation, and rose to his feet at the count of nine. He had gained just enough time—a precious few seconds—to recover. It was enough to get Tunney out of the woods, and he backpedaled for the rest of the round, taking more time to recuperate. In round eight, he lashed out and decked Dempsey. Dempsey rose, but the rest of the fight belonged to Tunney. By the final round, Dempsey had received considerable damage to his face by the continued punishment of Tunney's consistent, relentless jabs and was wobbling around the ring. Tunney went on to win the fight by decision. History has recorded this as the famous "Battle of the Long Count." It endures today as one of the greatest fight stories in boxing lore, and it has forever immortalized its heroes, Jack "Manassa Mauler" Dempsey and Gene "the Fighting Marine" Tunney—two men frozen forever in the lens of history over the exchange of mere seconds.

For Dempsey the loss was bittersweet. Again, he was more worshiped in defeat than victory. Tunney's image did not fare as well with the public at large—many, disliking his bookish intellectualism and literary circle of friends, remained vaguely suspicious of him—but more than anything else, many could never forgive him for upsetting Dempsey. Jack Dempsey never fought again, and retired at the age of 32 on March 4, 1928. In 1928, Gene married heiress Mary Josephine "Polly" Lauder. Gene had promised his prospective bride that he would retire from boxing, and he made good on his word, retiring in 1928 at the age of 31, and became a very successful businessman. Today, many people consider Gene Tunney to be one of the most underrated fighters in the history of the sport, overshadowed by those who fit the macho, tough-guy image most popular at the time. However one may judge his epic battles with Dempsey, Gene Tunney's record, determination, skills, and intellectual grasp of the sweet science elevate him amongst the greats in boxing history.

Their sensational battles in 1926 and 1927 tied them inextricably together for the rest of their lives. Tunney preceded Dempsey in death in 1978, and Dempsey was clearly saddened at the loss of his old nemesis. "When Dempsey learned of his old rival's death he said: 'We were as inseparable as Siamese twins. As long as Gene was alive, I felt we shared a link with that wonderful period of the past.'"[3] Later in his life, Gene Tunney was asked who was the best boxer in the first half of the twentieth century. He replied that Dempsey was the best fighter of all time. Since Tunney had beaten Dempsey twice, it begged the question of Tunney's true opinion on the subject. When Tunney was questioned on where he stood in the lineup, he declined to render an opinion. This final showing of diplomacy on the part of Gene Tunney does not mask the daunting challenge that both of these fighters unquestionably felt as they had stepped into the squared circle to face each other over 80 years ago.

Dempsey and Tunney helped each other take their own finely honed skills to a higher level and produced two of the most memorable boxing matches of the twentieth century.

But, ultimately, Dempsey and Tunney did more than achieve greatness in the ring. They proved that it is through competition that we challenge each other to truly test ourselves and our abilities. Regardless of the setting or circumstance, by teaming up, or competing with someone with excellent skills, preferably complementary to yours, you can pull abilities and strengths out of yourself which you could not achieve on your own. Simply put, competition is a means to attain the highest possible personal goals, and to challenge oneself to the limit, whether in a boxing ring, a corporate boardroom or any life endeavor.

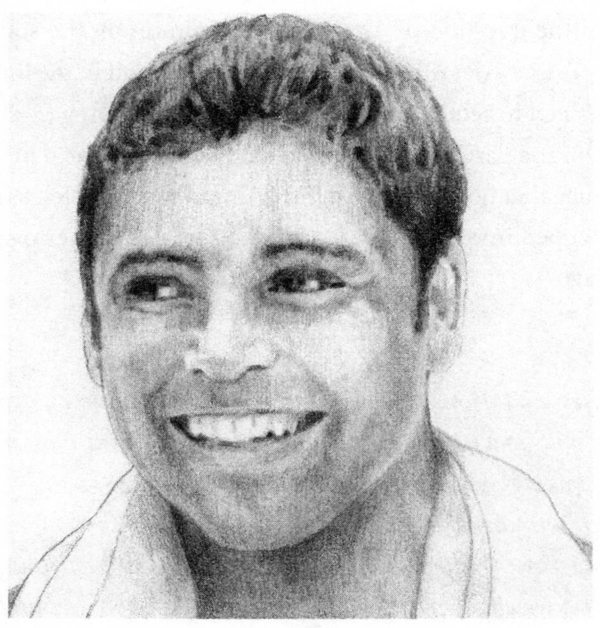

OSCAR DE LA HOYA

Born: February 4, 1973, East Los Angeles, CA

Won WBO Super Featherweight Title: March 5, 1994 (defeated Jimmy Bredahl)

Won vacant WBO Lightweight Title: July 29, 1994 (defeated Jorge Paez)

Won IBF Lightweight Title: May 6, 1995 (defeated Rafael Ruelas)

Won WBC Light Welterweight Title: June 7, 1996 (defeated Julio Cesar Chavez)

Won WBC Welterweight Title: April 12, 1997 (defeated Pernell Whitaker)

Lost WBC Welterweight Title: September 18, 1999 (Felix Trinidad)

Won WBC Super Welterweight Title: June 23, 2001 (defeated Javier Castillejo)

Won WBA Super Welterweight Title: September 14, 2002 (defeated Fernando Vargas)

Lost WBA Junior Middleweight and WBC Junior Middleweight Titles: September 13, 2003 (Shane Mosely)

Won WBO Middleweight Title: June 5, 2004 (defeated Felix Sturm)

Lost WBO Middleweight Title: September 18, 2004 (Bernard Hopkins)

Won WBC Super Welterweight Title: May 6, 2006 (defeated Ricardo Mayorga)

Lost WBC Super Welterweight Title: May 5, 2007 (Floyd Mayweather, Jr.)

Record: 39 wins, 6 losses, 30 knockouts

Boxing Handle: The Golden Boy

ROUND THREE

Challenging Yourself

✦ Oscar De La Hoya ✦

I realize I am a catalyst for the sport and I don't take that responsibility lightly. That is another reason I try to always compete at the highest level and give fans great fights by having match-ups with competition that gives me the most challenge and threat.

—Oscar De La Hoya

Oscar De La Hoya is an Olympic gold medalist who turned pro in 1992 and won titles across six different weight classes—a remarkable and unprecedented achievement in which he challenged himself again and again in a career in the ring that spanned two decades. However, while still champion and boxing actively, he successfully launched a number of business enterprises and became involved in significant philanthropic activities.

It is possible for a boxer to reach a peak in the sport where he has no real opposition in his particular weight class. A boxer can either stay in that comfort zone, or can move up or down to a different weight class where new, challenging opponents can be found. Boxers have a choice to avoid the tough fights, or they can look for them—to prove themselves.

As an example of a man who constantly searched for ways to better himself and the world in which he lives, De La Hoya has proven himself a true champion time and again.

✦ ✦ ✦

THE MIDDLE CHILD of Mexican immigrants, Oscar De La Hoya grew up in a rough neighborhood of East Los Angeles. Oscar's father, Joel De La Hoya, Sr., moved from Durango, Mexico, at the age of 16 and worked at a variety of jobs over his career, including grave digger, sheet-metal worker, machinist and shipping clerk. His mother, Cecilia Gonzalez, had a background in singing, and was visiting California on a visa while working in a zipper factory, when the couple met. The family had three children—in addition to Oscar are his older brother, Joel, Jr., and younger sister, Cecilia (Ceci).

Although the family was poor and often lived on food stamps, Oscar's parents frequently took the family to visit relatives in Mexico. Oscar relished these trips, which provided him with a very strong connection to his Mexican heritage. The trips also stuck with him because, despite the De La Hoya family's modest circumstances in East Los Angeles, they were perceived as if they were rich royalty coming from America where everyone was wealthy and prosperous.

In East L.A., the family lived in a tiny, second floor apartment, where Oscar shared a bedroom with his older brother. Gangs were a way of life in the neighborhood—shootings and muggings were not uncommon—and The Mexican Mafia also had a presence. Yet, despite their disadvantaged circumstances, the family was close and supportive of each other, and, as such, Oscar's world while growing up focused on his family.

The sport of boxing was a strong part of the De La Hoya family heritage, as Oscar's grandfather and father had both boxed as young men. Oscar's older brother also boxed. Although, as a little boy, Oscar preferred skateboarding and baseball, his brother and his father encouraged him to give boxing a try. Oscar had his first "bout" in his uncle's garage at the age of four and started boxing in the peewee circuit at the age of six. He followed a strict training routine, which included fighting no less than once a week, and sometimes traveled to neighboring towns to fight. At the age of 10, he reached amateur status.

Despite his young age, Oscar had a strong sense of what he wanted for his future. In the sixth grade, when assigned to write an essay, Oscar wrote that he wanted to be an Olympic gold medalist in boxing when he grew up. His classmates laughed at him and the teacher, who thought Oscar wasn't taking the assignment seriously, punished him by keeping him after class.

As Oscar grew, his father played a strong role in Oscar's training, emphasizing conditioning. For years, Oscar was awakened to go run every day at 4:30 in the morning by his father, who was leaving for work. By the time Oscar was a teenager, he had been training hard and was an impressive fighter. At 14, he was sparring with pros and holding his own, for five, six, even eight rounds, and would often draw a crowd to watch. As an amateur, Oscar compiled a solid record of 223 wins, 163 by knockout, with only 5 losses. He also won a number of championships, including the national Golden Gloves at 16 (119 pounds), the United States Amateur Championship at 17 (125 pounds), a gold medal in the 125-pound weight class at the 1990 Goodwill Games, and the 132-pound United States Amateur title one year later. As he increased in size and weight with age, he met every new challenge head on, and kept moving forward, constantly winning and improving.

But Oscar's accomplishments as a teenager were marked by tragedy: in 1990, when he was 17, his mother, Cecilia, who had been his inspiration in boxing and in life, passed away at the age of 39. An Olympic gold medal had always been her dream for her son, and following her death, Oscar renewed his commitment to honor her dream.

By 1991 when Oscar went to the world championships in Sydney, Australia, he hadn't lost a fight since 1987 and was favored to win the gold. However, he encountered a slick German fighter by the name of Marco Rudolph who outpointed him in a 17-13 decision. It was particularly painful, as this loss occurred right before the Olympic Games, but it was Oscar's vow to his mother to take gold that kept him on his Olympic path. Oscar qualified for the 1992 Barcelona games, where in the finals he again faced down Rudolph, who was favored to win over Oscar. Although the bout was hard fought and close, Oscar insured his victory by knocking down Rudolph in the final round to win a 7-2 decision. He was now an Olympic gold medalist in the lightweight division—the only American to bring home the gold medal in boxing from the Barcelona games. Oscar returned to East L.A. knowing that his mother would have been proud of him.

After entertaining offers from almost every major boxing promoter in the United States, Oscar went pro by signing with little known Robert Mittleman and Steve Nelson. They were offering a headline grabbing $1 million package, part of which Oscar was able to share with his father and former trainer. Oscar jumped almost immediately into the fray by winning his first pro fight with a first round KO over Lamar Williams on November 23, 1992.

Yet, despite the mountains he had climbed to reach this point in his career, his challenges as a professional boxer lay in front of him. He was ready. By 1996, when he squared off against Mexican legend Julio Cesar Chavez for the WBO Light Welterweight Championship, Oscar had already won World Super Featherweight and Lightweight Titles. Furthermore, upon entering the ring against Chavez, Oscar had an impressive record of 21-0 with 19 KO's. Yet Chavez was a long-standing and respected champion and had amassed an impressive record of 97-1 with one draw, along with several world titles. A true hero in his home country of Mexico, Chavez is generally accepted as one of the greatest fighters of his generation, and his 36 world title fights are the most in history. On June 7, 1996, Oscar showed the world that he had come of age as a true champion when he defeated Chavez by stopping him on cuts (facial cuts that were so severe that the fight could not continue without endangering Chavez) in four one-sided rounds. This victory over the iconic Chavez established Oscar as a legitimate champion and someone who could draw a sellout crowd. In addition, this was also De La Hoya's third weight class in which he had won a world championship.

Following the Chavez fight, Oscar fought regularly, continually challenging himself with the best in the business. He secured victories over boxing greats, among them Pernell Whitaker in 1997 (picking up the WBC Welterweight title, a championship in his fourth weight class) and Javier Castillejo in 2001 (picking up a title in his fifth weight class, the WBC Super Welterweight Title). These impressive victories were offset by losses to Felix Trinidad (1999) and Shane Mosely (2000).

Oscar gained more respect, especially from Hispanic fight fans, and cemented his ring reputation when he displayed true warrior instincts against Fernando Vargas in the championship fight for WBA and WBC Super-Welterweight titles, on September 14, 2002. Because Vargas had been very vocal about the upcoming fight with De La Hoya, questioning his ability, character, and even his heritage, the media began calling the fight "Bad Blood." The fight was an even match-up for the first half, but De La Hoya took control in the seventh round, and, in the eleventh round, unleashed a flurry of punches upon Vargas, who was trapped in the corner. This impressive TKO victory over Vargas helped him gain acceptance from the Hispanic community.

In 2003, Oscar defended his titles against Luis Ramon Camas, and then lost them to Shane Mosley. However, in 2004, he moved up in weight again by challenging Felix Sturm for the WBO Middleweight Title, and won a unanimous decision while capturing a title in a sixth weight class. This set the stage for one of the most important fights of his career: his World

Middleweight Championship bout against Bernard Hopkins, "The Executioner."

Hopkins was one of the biggest names in boxing, considered among the best pound-for-pound fighters in the world (a designation given to boxers who are the best overall, regardless of weight class). Oscar would take on Hopkins at the middleweight limit of 160 pounds, a weight class above which Oscar had been fighting for most his career, making this an even greater challenge for him. As a result, Hopkins was favored to win. When they squared off on September 18, 2004, for the World Middleweight Championship, Oscar overcame a cut on his left palm and fought a smart fight, leading on one of the judge's cards as the ninth round began. But Hopkins then hit him with a left hook to the liver, resulting in the first knockdown of Oscar's career. A well placed body shot to the liver can be devastating, and Oscar could not arise in time to beat the count. Despite this, De La Hoya made over $30 million from the fight. Once again, by taking on the best in the sport, Oscar lost no prestige in the boxing community, rather he proved that his motivation went beyond winning or earnings—his goal was to continually challenge himself, and his fans respected him for it.

It was to be almost two years before Oscar would fight again. In the meantime, his focus shifted to his business, and Oscar founded his own boxing promotion company, Golden Boy Promotions. On May 6, 2006, Oscar regained the WBC Super Welterweight Title by defeating Ricardo Mayorga and used the fight as an opportunity for Golden Boy Promotions to promote The Golden Boy himself. Over the years, in addition to Oscar himself, Golden Boy Promotions signed several top ranked boxers, including Bernard Hopkins and Shane Mosely, and also made them equity partners. Today, Golden Boy Promotions continues to flourish and is one of the premier promotional companies in boxing.

He then squared off against Floyd Mayweather, Jr., for the WBC Super Welterweight Title. One could say that Oscar was truly endeavoring to "go for the gold" by taking on an opponent with a phenomenal 37-0 record. At the time, Mayweather was universally considered the best pound-for-pound fighter in the world. On the fight date, May 5, 2007, De La Hoya pressed Mayweather round after round, but Floyd was awarded a split decision. Again, because of the excellent fight Oscar fought against someone who many considered the best in the world, his reputation for being a fighter unafraid to take the toughest challenges remained untarnished in spite of his loss. Promoted by Golden Boy Promotions, the fight earned the most of any fight in boxing history, generating nearly $700 million in pay-per-view income from 2.4 million viewers—surpassing the per-fight numbers generated by Mike Tyson's heavyweight match-ups with Evander Holyfield (two fights) and Lennox Lewis.

Oscar was to fight once more before retiring. Even in his last bout on December 6, 2008, Oscar faced yet another incredible hurdle in a seemingly invincible opponent, Manny Pacquiao, who brought a 47-3-2 record into the ring and *The Ring* magazine's designations as "2008 Fighter of the Year" and

"#1 Pound for Pound Fighter." In the end, Oscar was dealt a disappointing eight-round TKO loss. Still, he had proven, yet again, that no challenge was too formidable for the Golden Boy. Following the Pacquiao bout, Oscar retired from boxing on April 14, 2009.

Oscar De La Hoya's achievements in boxing are remarkable. Since turning pro in late 1992, De La Hoya won world titles in six different weight classes, the first person to ever do so. He was *The Ring* magazine's "Fighter of the Year" in 1995, and their top-rated "Pound for Pound" fighter in the world in 1997. He has also generated more money than any other boxer in the history of the sport and his crowd appeal has been unmatched, making record tickets sales and TV ratings. But what makes Oscar even more inspirational is that his drive to challenge himself has been so pervasive that it has led him to pursue success outside the ring. For some time prior to his retirement in boxing, he had been pursuing new challenges in the business world, and preparing himself for more.

Knowing that he needed help to smartly invest his sizable winnings from boxing, and fully realizing that he would likely be the subject of much bad advice by those who wanted to invest it for him or perhaps attempt to take advantage of him, De La Hoya actively cultivated a successful banker from a Swiss banking family, Richard Schaeffer. Richard had been working in the U.S. for a number of years and was deputy CEO of the private banking operation for UBS for the entire U.S., and the highest paid private banker in his company worldwide. Said Oscar, "'This is all too much for me,' I told Richard. 'I can't handle both my boxing career and the business side. I need a CEO for my financial interests, a quarterback to run the show.'"[1]

When Richard asked Oscar what his goals were, Oscar admitted that they were not modest: Oscar wanted nothing less than to build a business empire, using boxing promotion as a point of departure through Golden Boy Promotions, as that is what he knew best. From there, Oscar hoped to expand to other business ventures outside of boxing—real estate, media, sports teams, entertainment ventures and others. Oscar also saw the potential of the growing Hispanic buying power in the United States and felt that he, as a Mexican-American, had crossover appeal to both Anglo and Hispanic consumers. Through investing, Oscar also envisioned possible ways to help the Hispanic community.

With Richard Schaeffer on board, Golden Boy formed various investment companies in numerous business ventures. In 2003, they bought an office building on Madison Avenue in New York and sold it in 2006 at the height of the market, and acquired a high-rise on Wilshire Boulevard in downtown L.A., which now houses their offices. His investment companies have partnered with a Southern California developer to invest $100 million in commercial and residential properties in Hispanic communities. They have signed off on eight projects in locations ranging from California to Texas and encompassing everything from low-income housing to big-box construction. Other investments include interests in sports teams, including Golden Boy Mixed Martial Arts, and Houston Dynamo (a champion soccer team); Frontera Productions (a movie company geared to making films for Spanish-language audiences); various Hispanic newspapers; and Equal (the sugar substitute). There are also a number of other media and television interests, including ownership of *The Ring* (magazine). Plans for the hotel and leisure market, and the financial services industry, are currently underway.

Boxing is still at his roots, and eventually Oscar hopes to help his Golden Boy fighters become better prepared financially for their retirement from the ring, by offering them pensions, health insurance, and financial planning. In 1995 he started his own foundation, the Oscar De La Hoya Foundation, an organization dedicated to providing a better quality of life to the disadvantaged populations of East Los Angeles. He refurbished a gym and staffed it to train young fighters, one of whom became an Olympian, Jose Navarro, in the 2000 games in Sydney, Australia.

He established a cancer institute in his mother's honor, the Cecilia Gonzalez De La Hoya Cancer Center at White Memorial Medical Center, and opened the first new public high school in East Los Angeles in over 70 years, the Oscar De La Hoya Amino Charter High School, which is now ranked as one of the top 100 in the nation.

Those who have followed his career speculate that this determined boxing superstar will seek out even more opportunities in business and philanthropy. In a fitting tribute to the influence that he has had on the sport and from those who admire his commitment to challenging himself in and out of the ring, a seven-foot-tall bronze statue of Oscar De La Hoya was unveiled outside Staples Center in downtown Los Angeles on Monday, December 2, 2008. Today, De La Hoya's figure stands proud next to the statues of basketball great Magic Johnson and hockey legend Wayne Gretzky.

The story of Oscar De La Hoya has two important components—in the ring, and outside of it. In both arenas, he is living proof that continually challenging oneself to the next level in any endeavor can pay big dividends in the long run. Oscar De La Hoya has expanded his horizons and taken his career ever upward—first as a boxer, now as a businessman and philanthropist.

In boxing, as in life, it is easy to avoid the hard road ahead or languish after achievements. However, a true champion seizes every opportunity for a new challenge to move another rung up the ladder. One does not always get a second chance in life, so using challenges as opportunities to better one's life are key, and can pay off handsomely in the long run.

The remarkable achievements of this Olympic superstar, who is still on the "sunny side of 40," reflect the challenges he is willing to undertake and his constant search to better himself and the world in which he lives.

You have powers you never dreamed of. You can do things you never thought you could do. There are no limitations in what you can do except the limitations of your own mind.

—Darwin P. Kingsley, Former President of New York Life Insurance Company

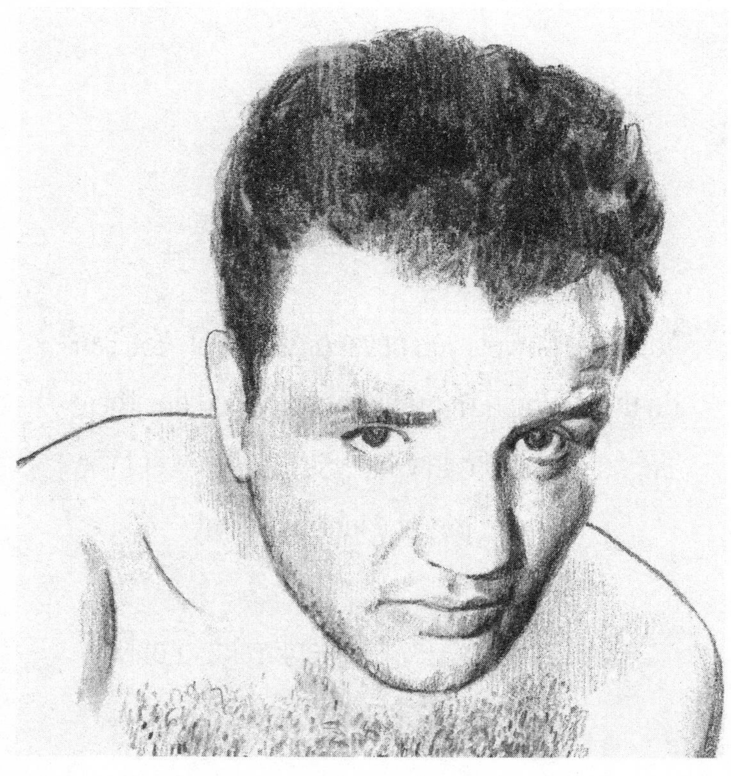

JAKE LAMOTTA

Born: July 10, 1922, Bronx, New York
Won World Middleweight Title: June 16, 1949 (defeated Marcel Cerdan)
Lost World Middleweight Title: February 14, 1951 ("Sugar" Ray Robinson)
Record: 83 wins, 19 losses, 4 draws, 30 knockouts
Boxing Handles: The Bronx Bull/The Raging Bull

ROUND FOUR

The Quality of Being Tough

✦ Jake LaMotta ✦

In his first 132 fights, he (Sugar Ray Robinson) was defeated only once, that by the redoubtable Jake LaMotta, the toughest middleweight I or anyone else ever saw.[1]

—Hall of Fame Referee Arthur Mercante

Jack LaMotta was tough as nails, and everyone knew it. Though he might have lacked some of the finesse or skills as some of his opponents, he would not surrender or retreat, no matter what he was up against. Anyone who took a fight with "the Bronx Bull" knew that they would be climbing into the ring with a man who refused to be knocked down or give up.

In boxing it can be an aura conveyed in the ring that truly sets a boxer apart—whether he wins or not. Toughness is one quality that sets champions apart, and it must be earned through fighting one's heart out and giving 100 percent effort at all times.

Like a bull in the ring, LaMotta fought hard from the beginning of the fight until the last bell and refused to go down. Although he didn't win every fight, his ability to stand his ground earned him respect from the crowd and critics alike, and cemented his reputation as a true champion.

✦ ✦ ✦

It can be said that any man is a product of his times. In the case of Jake LaMotta, the times were tough, and so was he. By any measure, Jake was as tough as they come.

Born in the New York City borough of the Bronx and raised by his Italian parents during the Depression, LaMotta's formative years were spent in tenement buildings and immigrant slums. He possessed an uncontrollable anger from as far back as he can remember. "When I was 8, I was already getting mad at people," he said. "I would clock them for talking to each other because I thought they might be talking about me. Sometimes I would get so crazy at nothing that I didn't give a damn what happened, whether I killed them or they killed me."[2] LaMotta himself did not know where this inborn anger came from; some of it was undoubtedly acquired from his father, who gave Jake an ice pick to defend himself when he was still a kid. It was not until Jake left his ice pick at home one day that he learned that he could defend himself with his fists. Jake's father capitalized on his son's talent by forcing him to fight other kids in the neighborhood for entertainment. The future world champion was rewarded for his efforts with pennies, nickels and dimes thrown into the ring; these small earnings helped pay the rent. It is estimated that LaMotta had hundreds of street fights in his formative years. By the time he was a teen, LaMotta had learned two important lessons: that he could box, and that there was money to be made by doing so.

In his formative years, Jake robbed people for money and

goods, often teaming up with his boyhood friend and future boxing champion Rocky Graziano. Later, Rocky recalled, "Me and Jake really weren't so bad . . . we only stole things that began with the letter 'A'—A wallet . . . A radio . . . A car."[3] However, when Jake was 17, he attempted to rob a local bookie at one o'clock in the morning. When Jake struck the bookie on the back of the head and the man didn't go down right away, LaMotta lost control and beat the man savagely. Jake fled from the scene with the man's wallet but was never tracked down by the police. However, the incident carried other repercussions for Jake. The next day, a newspaper incorrectly reported that the bookie had died from his wounds. The knowledge that he killed a man haunted LaMotta for years. Although La Motta would eventually learn that the reporter had made an error in reporting the story and that the bookie had lived, LaMotta spent much of his career taking punches to punish himself for this "sin" of killing another man. Some speculate that, during his career, LaMotta's seeming lack of fear and eagerness to absorb pain in the ring was in fact self-repentance. Photos later taken of him during the 40's show him to be wistful, introspective and aloof, almost detached from the present. Perhaps that night, when he was only 17, helps explain the blank stares he so often adopted in front of the boxing public in later years.

Not long after his encounter with the bookie, LaMotta tried to rob a jewelry store and was caught by the police. He was sent away to a notorious reform school in Coxsackie, N.Y., where he was reacquainted with his friend Rocky Graziano. As this stage of their lives, Graziano and LaMotta could have hardly known that both would later become World Middleweight Champions, and have movies made about themselves.

LaMotta began his pro career as a light heavyweight in 1941 at the age of 19. From his first fight, it was clear he was as scrappy and rugged as they come; a rough and tumble fighter who fought with anger and determination. For him, each fight was a personal war, and he would take no prisoners. Jake sported a granite-like jaw which could take the punishment of anything thrown at him. He fought in a crouch-like style, and his entire offensive strategy was directed at his opponent's body. He was not known for his knockout ability, but his superhuman endurance and bull-like style would gradually wear his opponents down. He had good punching power, and was known for his "bully" style of boxing, where he would stay physically close to his opponent, absorbing punches, and would stalk his adversary around the ring looking for a chance to land his own hard shots. His boxing style reflected his own personality—straight ahead, street-like, unrelenting slugging and brawling, with little finesse or grace. All of this came with a tremendous will to win.

Jake prided himself on his ability to withstand any punch and stay on his feet. He quickly won his first 15 professional fights and earned the nickname "The Bronx Bull." Said LaMotta "That was because of the way I fought—charge out of the corner, punch, punch, punch, never give up, take all the punishment the other guy could hand out but stay in there, slug and slug and slug."[4] This strategy served him well: in his 13 year career as a professional boxer, he was knocked down only once in 106 bouts.

On October 2, 1942, when LaMotta was 20 years old, he had earned the chance to fight Sugar Ray Robinson, considered by many to be the best pound-for-pound fighter of the twentieth century. Although this was their first fight, it wouldn't be their last; the two would meet six times over eight years. During this first fight, LaMotta hung in for 10 rounds but Robinson was ultimately the victor, winning by unanimous decision. Their second meeting, another 10 rounder, took place less than a year later, on February 5, 1943, and this time LaMotta knocked Robinson through the ropes in the eighth round and was awarded the win by unanimous decision. In doing so, LaMotta had the distinction of delivering Robinson his first professional career loss. Although Robinson would out-box LaMotta during their next three fights, their fights were wars and always went the 10 round distance. In their fifth 10-round encounter, Robinson gained a split decision, but afterwards said "this was the toughest fight I've ever had with LaMotta." There was one last bout on their horizon but, in the meantime, LaMotta had another battle to fight, outside of the ring: he had to contend with the Mafia.

The forties were a difficult time to be a boxer. The Mafia played a key role, and many fighters were forced to hand over large portions of purses to prevent problems for themselves, and also to insure that they were able to get fights. For his part, LaMotta avoided contact with the criminal underworld as long as he could. But this had consequences. Despite his impressive performance against Robinson and other top fighters of the day, the opportunity to fight for the title was kept from LaMotta (he had been frozen out of any chance at a championship fight because he wouldn't appoint anyone from the underworld as his manager). Finally, after fighting seven years as a leading contender without a hint of a title shot, LaMotta finally concluded that he would have to play ball with the "mob" if he ever wanted a chance at a championship belt. With his record standing at 65-11-3, LaMotta agreed to throw a bout against Billy Fox in exchange for a title shot.

On November 14, 1947, LaMotta stepped into the ring prepared to lose to Fox. Billy Fox was a light heavyweight with an impressive 49-1 record and 49 knockouts, and LaMotta rationalized that losing to Fox would not affect LaMotta's status as a middleweight contender. However, when it came to the actual contest, LaMotta's pride refused to let him take a fall without putting up a fight. Characteristically as tough as ever, LaMotta was rough on Fox in the early going, but then stood on the ropes in the fourth round and took a myriad of punches—punches that he couldn't answer since he had a "deal" to let Fox win. Referee Frank Fullam called a halt to the bout toward the end of round four. In addition to adding a loss to his record, LaMotta had to pay the Mafia $20,000. With his background from the streets of New York, LaMotta took the Fox match in stride; he knew paying his dues to the boxing landlords of the day was his only road to a championship belt. Nevertheless, it was a frustrating time for LaMotta, as he still had to wait two years for his title shot.

On June 16, 1949, LaMotta's chance at the title finally came. He was up against World Middleweight Champion Marcel Cerdan, considered by many fight critics to be Europe's greatest fighter at that time. Many thought Cerdan had boxing skills superior to those of LaMotta. In round one, LaMotta wrestled Cerdan to the ground, and Cerdan fell heavily on his back, tearing a muscle in his left shoulder. With this injury which impaired the use of his left arm, Cerdan tried his best, but could not beat LaMotta with only one arm. Cerdan retired after the ninth round. At last, LaMotta was now Middleweight Champion of the World. When his victory was announced, Jake's tough guy image dissolved in a single moment. He threw his arms around his wife, Vikki, and cried. LaMotta described this moment as the happiest of his life.

With his new championship title, Jake's popularity accelerated as the 40's ended. His bull-like style, possum-playing craftiness, and "take no prisoners" mentality gave him renewed box office appeal. Jake was a clever boxer in many ways, more so than history often gives him credit for. He was strategic and would roll with the punches to minimize their impact. He frequently "played possum" in the ring, pretending to tire and leaning on the ropes like a defeated fighter—only to suddenly spring forth with a barrage of unexpected punches that would surprise and dismantle his opponent. These ring tactics appealed to the crowd, and they loved Jake. From before the first bell, he put on a good show; superstitious, he would never enter the ring without his leopard-skin robe. Outside of the ring, his turbulent personal life often made the news; his violent nature defined his relationship with Vikki, who was his second wife and a strikingly beautiful woman who would later model for *Playboy* in her fifties. LaMotta was a classic tough-guy—of course, nowhere was that more clear than inside the ring. On September 13, 1950, when he faced down French fighter Laurent Dauthuille who brought a 36-8-2 record into the ring, LaMotta would once again prove how far being tough could get him.

For the first 14 rounds, Dauthuille dominated in the ring, easily out pointing and frustrating LaMotta. However, the fifteenth round witnessed one of the greatest reversals in championship boxing. Though LaMotta was losing the round (and the fight), he hung in there, and in round 15, finally caught Dauthuille with a tremendous punch thrown in sheer desperation. LaMotta followed this with a barrage of punches and a devastating left hook that closed the show. With only 13 seconds left on the clock, LaMotta won by knockout, retaining his Middleweight Championship. By refusing to accept defeat, LaMotta again defined himself as one of the toughest fighters of all time. For his showing of true heart and courage, LaMotta must be credited for this fight being chosen as *The Ring* magazine's "fight of the decade," and, over two decades later, the 'greatest come from behind victory' in their 1977 "75th Anniversary" awards.[5]

On February 14, 1951, he and Sugar Ray Robinson fought their sixth and final match in what boxing history now refers to as the "St. Valentine's Day Massacre." This championship fight is considered by many boxing historians to be one of the best of all time, largely because of LaMotta's resilience and bravery, and refusal to give up, despite the tremendous beating he received from Robinson in the later rounds. By round

13, LaMotta, exhausted and hanging on the ropes, was clearly beaten by Robinson. Still, the Bronx Bull refused to be knocked down by Robinson despite the tremendous barrage of punches Robinson continued to throw at him. As blood was spurting and flashbulbs were popping, LaMotta won over the crowd that night with his guts, and sheer will and determination, even though Robinson won the fight by referee stoppage and captured LaMotta's Middleweight Crown. As Robinson celebrated his well-deserved victory, it was LaMotta who was elevated to boxing immortality.

LaMotta retired in 1954. By that time, he bore many war wounds of his chosen profession, including a nose that had been broken six times, and a marriage that eventually didn't make it (Jake and Vikki divorced in 1957). But LaMotta remained as tough as ever. In 1960, when LaMotta was asked to testify at a hearing of a Senate investigation into corruption in boxing, he didn't back down. Although LaMotta had been criticized for his participation in mob-related activities, and his reputation had suffered for it, he felt that it was important he speak out about the realities of the fight game. When asked at the hearing if he felt any threat from the mob, LaMotta bellowed "I'm not afraid of none of them rats."[6] LaMotta's testimony proved to be very important in aiding the authorities, but, more so, his participation and defiance was symbolic of his toughness and willingness to stand up to anyone.

After his gloves were hung up for the last time, LaMotta was still a figure in popular culture. Following retirement, he moved to Miami, opened a club, and dated a number of Hollywood starlets, Ginger Rogers, Jayne Mansfield and Jane Russell among them. He became a stand-up comedian and appeared in over 15 movies, including *The Hustler*, with Paul Newman (Jake played the bartender.) A black and white film entitled *Raging Bull*, based on Jake's life, was made in 1980. Directed by Martin Scorsese, the film received seven Academy Award nominations, and is considered to be one of the best boxing movies of all time. Robert DeNiro, who played LaMotta and was trained by Jake in preparation for the fight scenes, received the Best Actor award.

LaMotta's deserved tough guy image served him well in the ring and has also worked for him in his post-boxing life, as he carried that image onto the stage and his other activities in a more playful and non-threatening way, after his gloves were hung up for the last time. Today, LaMotta is in his late 80's and was frequently seen around New York City in his trademark black cowboy hat, attending various boxing and celebrity events, prior to his move to Miami in July 2009. Defiant and outspoken as always, yet mellowed, LaMotta is always engaging, and is eager to launch into his stand-up comic routine. For Jake, it was his toughness, borne of his time in the ring and solidified, punch-after-punch, that made all of the difference.

Jake LaMotta embodied "tough" in a tough sport. It was his reputation as "tough" that earned him respect in and out of the ring, and fostered his legendary status as a boxer.

In any endeavor in life, it is much the same. Tough is a dimension of strength and granite-like hardness that means someone won't walk away from a fight when what matters is on the line. Tough doesn't necessarily mean bad, or mean; it means one has earned a reputation that he or she can not be pushed around. This reputation can be a tremendous asset and help someone achieve any goal, sometimes by sheer intimidation and reputation. Although the toughest guy doesn't always win, he/she is always respected, and in this way, toughness can be the extra edge to help someone overcome any odds and succeed, whether in the "squared ring" or behind an executive's desk, a maestro's podium, or the corporate boardroom.

Being tough is a badge of honor.

GEORGE FOREMAN

Born: January 10, 1949, Marshall, Texas
Won WBA and WBC Heavyweight Titles: January 22, 1973 (defeated Joe Frazier)
Lost WBA and WBC Heavyweight Title: October 30, 1974 (Muhammad Ali)
Inactive: March 17, 1977 to March 9, 1987
Won IBF and WBA Heavyweight Titles: November 5, 1994 (defeated Michael Moorer
Lost IBF and WBA Heavyweight Titles: November 22, 1997 (Shannon Briggs)
Record: 76 wins, 5 losses, 68 knockouts
Boxing Handle: Big George

ROUND FIVE

Reinventing Yourself and Making a Comeback

✦ George Foreman ✦

> In any listing of great comebacks, the finger of history lingers longer over the name of George Foreman than any figure in boxing—nay, all of sports.[1]
>
> —Bert Randolph Sugar

After a devastating loss to Muhammad Ali in 1974 and an unexpected defeat from Jimmy Young in 1977, George Foreman retired from boxing at the age of 28 and reinvented himself as a Protestant minister. After a decade outside of the ring, in which he changed his image from a fierce, angry, hulking brute to a friendlier, more likeable easy-going guy, he decided to make a comeback—far beyond the age when most boxers retire. Against all odds, he followed his dream and successfully reclaimed the World Heavyweight Title.

Boxing is a tough, demanding sport, and it is common for even the greatest of champions to lose more than one fight during their career. Many a great boxer is knocked to the canvas, injured, or receives an unexpected upset. It is how someone "picks themselves off the canvas" and forges ahead that defines a champion.

The story of George Foreman, with his failures and setbacks, followed by reinvention, re-emergence and triumph, defines the meaning of "comeback kid," and is a classic in the annals of sports, business and life.

✦ ✦ ✦

GEORGE FOREMAN WAS born in a poor community in Marshall, Texas, the fifth child of seven. His father, J.D., was a railroad construction worker who was largely absent and drank away much of his earnings. Shortly after George was born, George's mother, Nancy Ree, moved the family to Houston in search of work where she raised her seven children almost single-handedly.

George grew up on the mean streets of Houston's Fifth Ward, known as the "Bloody Fifth" because of the frequent knifings associated with street fights and neighborhood crime. As a boy, George was bigger and stronger than most boys and violence was second nature to him: he would provoke fights with anyone, anywhere, for any reason, as often as two or three times a day. George never lost a fight and took pride in his macho reputation. His skills as a fighter also drew him close to his father. Despite his frequent absence, J.D. Foreman had great faith in his son, and believed from the get-go that young George would become a champion boxer. George's father would say, "Heavyweight champion of the world, . . . Stronger than Jack Johnson. Hits like Jack Dempsey."[2] Though George did not recognize those names, he appreciated his father's enthusiasm and admiration. Still, aside from forging a connection with his father, George's life was headed nowhere. Increasingly, he became involved in mugging, street fighting, petty theft and drinking.

At the age of 15, he woke up one day and realized that he was a thug, and well on his way to becoming a criminal. Shocked by this revelation, he resolved never to steal again. Unfortunately, his change of heart came a little too late; after failing most of his classes and ditching school, George dropped out before he completed junior high. Barely able to read or write, he did not know what to do with his life. All he had was his tough guy image, which he had fostered so carefully.

Then, in 1965, at age 16, George saw something that changed his life. Miraculously, George was watching television when he saw a commercial about the Job Corps, a program established by President Lyndon B. Johnson to provide work and hope for no-hope problem kids like George. George realized this was his only chance at turning his life around, so he signed up. George was sent out of state to live at a Corps training center in Oregon, and later, California. These were eye-opening journeys for a young man who had rarely been anywhere. At the Corps, George was finally educated in a way that worked for him, and as someone who had never read a book before arriving in Oregon, he jumped at the chance to improve his vocabulary by reading everything he could get his hands on. Today, George credits his participation in the Job Corps with having turned his life around. George earned his high school equivalency diploma and gained practical knowledge in forestry and construction. At the Corps, George was also introduced to the sport of boxing. George soon found that boxing managed to calm the rage he had always possessed. The sport also granted him confidence and independence; at last, he felt he was someone who could stand firmly on his own two feet. And he was good at boxing—really good.

Once George began to box on the amateur circuit, he advanced quickly, as his size, strength and power made him an instant success. In 1968, he won the national amateur boxing title at the Amateur Athletic Union (AAU) tournament in Toledo, Ohio. Thereafter, he terminated his training in the Job Corps and joined the Olympic boxing team to compete in Mexico City for the Olympic Games that year. Less than two years after his first boxing match, he defeated the Soviet finalist Jonas Cepulis in two rounds and captured the Olympic gold medal in the Heavyweight Division. Wrapping up his amateur career with a record of 27-0, Foreman turned pro.

Upon his return to Texas, George met Sonny Liston and soon became a full-time member of Liston's camp. In Liston, Foreman had one of the best sparring partners he could have wished for. Although Liston would die one year later at the age of 38, in their short time together, Liston made a lasting impression on the up-and-coming Foreman. Among other things, Liston's cold, steely, nearly silent demeanor stuck with George. Then George met two other famous athletes, basketball great Walt Frazier and football legend Jim Brown, both of whom reacted in a lukewarm manner to the young, enthusiastic boxer. Based on the reception he got from Walt Frazier and Jim Brown, George decided that a stoic, threatening, tough-guy image was the best way for a successful athlete to conduct himself. From that point forward, Foreman's Liston-inspired stare, combined with his hulking presence in the ring, sent chills down the backs of even the most loyal fans. Never smiling, he was feared and unpopular. In his interviews with the press, he would frequently answer with "yep" and "nope," behavior that contributed to his unpopularity in the public eye. In later years, George would say that, if Jim Brown and Walt Frazier had treated him more cordially, he would have adopted a friendlier disposition.

Despite his negative public reception, George enjoyed much success when he turned pro, quickly running up a string of 37 victories—34 by knockout—with no defeats. By 1973, George had earned himself a title shot against World Heavyweight Champ "Smokin' Joe" Frazier, a powerful boxer with a 29-0, 25 KO record who also had the impressive accomplishment of having defeated Muhammad Ali. When they fought on January 22, 1973, George dramatically defeated Frazier in a second round TKO, knocking him down six times. The final knockdown was a massive uppercut which lifted Frazier up off the canvas with the sheer force of the blow. George was now Heavyweight Champion of the World, 38-0, with 35 knockouts. After he demolished Frazier, the word "invincible" was also used to describe him, further enhancing his image as an indestructible and sinister force in the ring.

Foreman successfully defended his title in two quick knockouts of challengers King Roman and Ken Norton, setting the stage for what was to be a defining moment of his career: the

"Rumble in the Jungle" against Muhammad Ali. On October 30, 1974, Ali challenged Foreman for his titles in Kinshasa, Zaire, in what history has labeled one of the most exciting and dramatic heavyweight fights ever. Simply outwitted by Ali in the contest and knocked out in the eighth round, Foreman was no longer viewed as invincible, and a long road lay ahead of him before he would wear a heavyweight championship belt again. The fact that he failed to get off the canvas that night, believing to himself that he could have, would haunt him in the years that followed. The loss he suffered in Zaire on that early African morning became an indelible mark on his record that was to define and ultimately change his life.

After this loss, Foreman spent the next two years fighting exhibitions. Then on March 17, 1977, he squared off against Jimmy Young in San Juan, Puerto Rico. Foreman fought hard for 12 rounds, but his energy flagged in the later rounds and Young won by decision. Exhausted and despondent, Foreman fell ill in his dressing room. It was then that something happened to change Foreman's life: there, in the dressing room, Foreman experienced a spiritual revelation. Following this epiphany, Foreman became a born-again Christian and retired from boxing that year at the age of 28.

Foreman went back to Houston a changed man. He let go of his driving anger and devoted himself to his family and his religion, becoming an ordained minister in 1978. He loved to preach, and his life story and celebrity status (which he tried to downplay) made him a very popular minister. Foreman also preached on some of the same street corners where, years earlier, he used to mug and steal. Foreman made significant lifestyle changes as well. He cut his hair, eventually shaved his head, gave up his luxury cars as well as several houses, and stopped watching television and flying first class. He also gave up exercising, ate whatever he wanted, and gained a lot of weight. And unlike the "old" George Foreman, he started smiling. In 1981, Foreman built his own church in a suburb of Houston called Humble, into which he poured his energies and resources, along with his own money.

Over the course of the next few years, George married several times and had 10 children, five girls and five boys. All five of his sons are named George Edward Foreman, each with the addition of a Roman numeral and a nickname. George's decision to name all of his sons after himself was also not as whimsical or ego-driven as one might conclude; deeply affected in his youth by his father's absence, George wanted to give each of his sons the gift of his heritage, one that could not be taken away from him. One of his daughters is named Georgette.

In 1983, Foreman, along with his brother Reid, founded the George Foreman Youth and Community Center in Houston to keep young people away from drugs and crime by establishing facilities to encourage participation in sports and learning. Four years after its founding, George realized the center needed more funds. So, after a 10-year hiatus, George decided to go back into boxing. Foreman's return to the ring in 1987 was marked with great skepticism. He was now 37 years old, way past the age that most fighters retire. What's more, he was now a gentler, humbler man.

Many people viewed George's return to the ring as a publicity stunt; others derided his efforts. Not only did Foreman look out of shape, but, in order to supplement his income, he became a pitchman for hamburgers and other fast food, and often joked of his huge appetite. His image had been transformed to a smiling, friendly, bald-headed, almost touchy-feely, "teddy bear" type of person, a far cry from his earlier moody, surly self. It was hard for boxing fans to believe that he could have much to offer inside the ropes. Still, George was determined to challenge himself, and also wanted to show the whole world that his age didn't matter.

On March 9, 1987, George stepped into the ring for the first time in over a decade to take on a boxer named Steve Zouski. George weighed in at 267 pounds and appeared badly out of shape. But George easily defeated Zouski, winning by a fourth round TKO. George's lifetime record was now 46-2. Many victories followed against younger, fitter fighters, mostly by knockout. But it wasn't until Foreman squared up against former top heavyweight contender and big puncher, Gerry Cooney, that the boxing world began to really take notice of his return to the ring as a serious contender. On January 15, 1990, in Atlantic City, to the amazement of many, Foreman handed Cooney a second round knockout, bringing his lifetime record to 65-2. Every penny he made was sent back to the George Foreman Youth and Community Center.

Foreman then racked up four more wins by knockout, bringing his record since his comeback to 24 wins and no losses, including 23 knockouts, and had slowly earned respect from boxers and the press. Now widely viewed as a true contender to regain the Heavyweight Title, he challenged Evander Holyfield for the Undisputed Heavyweight Crown on April 19, 1991. With a record of 25-0 at the time, Holyfield was also an Olympic gold medalist who had gained the Undisputed Heavyweight Crown six months earlier by knocking out Buster Douglas, the man who had dethroned Mike Tyson.

In a hard fought contest watched by 1.4 million pay-per-view viewers, George displayed two characteristics which had been heretofore absent in his former career—a world-class jab and the patience to use it. His jab now dominated his offense in contrast to his former career where he had relied almost solely on his big right hand. Though the crowds were on his side, Big George struggled against a faster, sharper, and obviously younger champion, but was nevertheless able to go the distance. Winning by a unanimous decision, Holyfield said afterwards he had laced Foreman with everything he had and could not fell him. Foreman was only to comment, "He won the points, but I proved the point."[3] Following this fight, George fully endowed the youth center with the proceeds from his winnings. Foreman won three other fights before losing in a WBO title match by decision to Tommy Morrison on June 7, 1993, in a fight that he felt he had won.

Holyfield was to lose his WBA and IBF titles by decision to Michael Moorer on April 22, 1994, and George was given another chance to become champion. With an impressive lifetime record of 72-4, George emerged from his dressing room to greet Moorer and nearly 14,000 people at the MGM

Grand Garden in Las Vegas on November 5, 1994, twenty years after his loss to Ali. On his spirited jog to the ring that night, Foreman was accompanied by Sam Cooke's music "If I Had a Hammer," and the applause turned into a deafening roar when he climbed between the ropes into the ring. It was Big George's shining moment, and everyone in attendance grasped its significance. Wearing the same trunks that he had worn in Zaire 20 years earlier, once a bright red but now faded to pink, Foreman entered the ring as a substantial underdog.

As the fight progressed, it appeared that it was all for naught for Foreman. For nine impressive rounds, Moorer hammered away at the older, slower challenger, pummeling him with a steady right jab, accompanied by solid left and right punches that rocked Foreman time and again. All the while, George's left eye was continuing to swell, and exhaustion appeared to be taking its toll. Then, out of nowhere in the tenth round, George uncorked a combination to Moorer's head, followed by a thundering, short straight right which landed squarely on the chin of Moorer knocking him down and out, and Foreman again into boxing history, as he had made believers out of everyone by reclaiming his Heavyweight World Title at the age of 45.

Now the oldest man to ever win the World Heavyweight Crown, Foreman went back to his corner and knelt in prayer as the arena erupted in cheers and absolute mayhem. His success touched all corners of the arena—the chest of every man who was middle-aged and older swelled with pride, living vicariously through George's amazing accomplishment. Younger admirers were equally proud, marveling at what he had done.

The once-young, brooding, defiant man who had *alienated* the crowd had become the transformed, positive, congenial middle-aged champion who *owned* the crowd. In every sense of the word, his comeback was complete.

A few other bouts followed. After losing a controversial decision to Shannon Briggs on November 22, 1997, in a bout he thought he had won, Foreman announced his "final" retirement from boxing shortly thereafter at the age of 48.

The story does not end here. Following his successful "second coming"—and going —in boxing, he went on to become a very successful boxing analyst and announcer for HBO. His most successful business venture was his promotion of the George Foreman Lean Mean Fat Reducing Grilling Machine, where he has said that he earned more than he had in his entire boxing career. George does not dispute that his earnings as a product promoter are over $200 million, several times what he is estimated to have earned in the ring. He has written several books, and has other successful business interests and media ventures.

Thirty-five years after The Rumble in the Jungle, George Foreman is a man at peace with himself and on top of the world. One might speculate that it was his loss to Ali that brought him down to earth, and caused him to reevaluate himself and his purpose. He ultimately gained the inner strength to take a step to the side, loop around, and then reemerge with the grit and determination of a true champion, his image remade, likeable and appealing. From there he was able to pull off one of the greatest miracles in all of sports, and amass a fortune. All the while, the George Foreman Youth and Community Center has continued to help people get in shape and improve their lives.

George Foreman's story as a "comeback" champion makes him stand very tall and extremely respectable in any list of boxing greats. Furthermore, his comeback, accompanied by his successful reinvention of himself, serves to underscore the grit, determination, resolve and cunning of this modern day hero, both in and out of the ring.

Today, in addition to his impressive championship record as a boxer, George Foreman's new image has helped him become a successful and wealthy businessman, and television sports announcer.

Sometimes the best solution for someone who has experienced losses, difficulties or defeats in their lives is to "take a break," "try something new," or "reinvent themselves." A change can present new opportunities. Or, as in the case of George Foreman, taking time off and then giving another try at what initially made him successful, perhaps approaching it in a different way the second time, can provide a renewed opportunity to succeed, i.e., to "make a comeback." The lessons of George Foreman can be applied to so many of life's circumstances—in business, in politics, or in following a passion like acting, music or writing.

Not everyone gets it right the first time. Attempting a comeback or a makeover can be the best thing that can happen to someone—as we can all learn, in spades, from George Foreman.

Life is like boxing. You've only got so many punches to throw, and you can only take so many.

—George Foreman

JAMES J. BRADDOCK

Born: June 7, 1905, New York City
Died: November 29, 1974, North Bergen, New Jersey
Won World Heavyweight Title: June 13, 1935 (defeated Max Baer)
Lost World Heavyweight Title: June 22, 1937 (Joe Louis)
Record: 51 wins, 26 losses, 7 draws, 2 no-contests, 26 knockouts
Boxing Handle: James J. Braddock

ROUND SIX

Overcoming Obstacles / Persistence and Determination

✦ James J. Braddock ✦

Never, never, never, never give up.

—Winston Churchill

James J. Braddock grew up poor, succeeded as a boxer early in his life, fell from grace in the ring, and struggled to provide food and shelter for his family during the Great Depression—yet he still became a champion. Small in size for a heavyweight, with hands that broke often, Braddock seemed to have everything against him. However, he never gave up, and while wandering the city looking for work as a longshoreman or any other job that might put food on the table, he persevered. Braddock fought back to win what many view as the most prestigious prize in sports, the Heavyweight Championship of the World.

Though Braddock's example is extreme, becoming a successful boxer is never easy. Due to the intensity and inherent danger in the sport, there are unique challenges and stumbling blocks which any fighter must overcome.

Over seventy years later, Braddock's story remains an inspiration today, and demonstrates that an iron will and a determined spirit can make up for almost any obstacle one might encounter.

JAMES WALTER BRADDOCK was born in a tiny tenement apartment in Hell's Kitchen in New York City to Joseph Braddock and Elizabeth O'Toole, both immigrants from the Manchester area of Ireland. James Walter, the sixth of seven children, tipped the scales at his very first weigh-in: moments after entering the world, the doctor recorded his weight at an incredible 17½ pounds. At the time of Jimmy's birth, Hell's Kitchen was the center of Irish life in New York City, but a dirty and dangerous place overrun with vicious street gangs. Shortly after Jimmy was born, the family moved across the Hudson River to West New York, New Jersey, to escape the filthy and unsafe conditions of the city.

Like most boys, little Jimmy Braddock enjoyed playing marbles and baseball, swimming in the Hudson River, and dreamed of becoming a fire fighter or train engineer. He also had the tendency to get into street fights, a habit that he had plenty of opportunities to indulge at St. Joseph's Parochial School where he traded punches with his schoolmates on a daily basis. Jimmy's tendency to get in trouble, combined with a lack of interest in academics, ended his school career early, and he dropped out at the age of 14.

With few vocational qualifications or skills, Braddock had limited career choices. From 1919 until 1923, he worked a series of jobs, including a Western Union messenger boy, typesetter, an errand boy for a silk mill, and a teamster. It was during this time that Braddock discovered his propensity to fight translated well into the sport of boxing. After sparring a few times and learning that he could hold his own with almost anyone, Braddock was hooked. He loved the feeling of winning and the boost to his self-esteem that came with gaining people's respect through his victories.

Braddock entered the circuit of amateur boxing in 1924, at the age of 18, and spent the next two years honing his skills with more than 100 amateur fights. He proved to be good with his fists, with a hard punch and granite chin. With his fighter's instinct to inflict pain, he quickly developed a reputation as a force to be reckoned with and the amateur boxing world began to take notice of this promising upstart. From 1924–1926, he virtually tore through the amateur ranks of New Jersey, ascending to the championship round with ease. In a blaze of glory that amazed all who witnessed it, he won the state's amateur Light Heavyweight Championship in 1925 in a fight that lasted less than two minutes; then, he fought for the amateur Heavyweight Championship of New Jersey only two nights later, and won—again, in less than two minutes. The 19-year-old Braddock was now New Jersey's amateur Heavyweight *and* Light Heavyweight Champion, and it was soon time for the 6'2½" Braddock to turn pro, capitalize on his boxing skills, and make some money.

In 1926, at the age of 20, Jimmy entered the pro circuit as a light heavyweight. Not long after his first pro bout, Braddock met Joe Gould, the manager who was to guide him throughout his professional career. Gould, a dapper, debonair, cigar-puffing manager and businessman, was savvy and worked hard to make Braddock a big name in boxing. At Gould's suggestion, Braddock fought under the name "James J. Braddock", ostensibly to follow a pattern set by former World Heavyweight Champions James J. Jeffries, James J. Corbett and James J. Tunney (known as "Gene"). Despite a slow start (Braddock's first fight was a no decision draw), Braddock soon begin tearing through his opponents, knocking out most of them. In his first year, Braddock won 13 fights out of 15 including 12 by knockout (eight of those knockouts occurred in the first round). Since the other two fights ended in draws, he had not technically lost any fights. Now Braddock was well on his way in his new professional boxing career. Already, his knockout power made him a popular fighter. Outside of the ring, Gould wined and dined promoters, writers and other people of influence in the boxing world, talking up the boxing prowess of his promising young prospect. All of this placed Braddock prominently in the public eye and enhanced his image as an up-and-coming young boxer.

On November 30, 1928, Braddock was matched against a well respected and very skilled fighter, Tuffy Griffiths, who sported a perfect record of 36-0 with 22 knockouts. Jimmy, who was a seven to one underdog going into the fight, administered a TKO in the second round, dropping Tuffy four times in the bout. This win caused a sensation in the boxing world. Braddock was now recognized in public places, and crowds gathered to watch and admire him when he worked out at the famous Stillman's Gym in New York City. When Braddock was seen at Stillman's or went out on the town, fans clamored for the chance to shake the hand of the man who had defeated Tuffy Griffiths. In a newspaper article, former Heavyweight Champion Gene Tunney predicted that Braddock would someday win the heavyweight title. When the February 1929 issue of *The Ring* magazine hit the stands, Braddock graced the cover with the caption "Jimmy Braddock, One of the World's Great Heavyweights."

In July 1929, 24 year old Braddock was given a shot at the Light Heavyweight Title, when he was matched against champion Tommy Loughran at Yankee Stadium. By this time, Braddock had lost only three fights out of 46 contests. Loughran, known as "The Phantom of Philly," was a true master of the sweet science and was viewed by many as one of the most talented boxers in history. A boxer who believed in preparation and the importance of technique, Loughran had been floored only four times out of his first 117 fights and had never been knocked out. Loughran was a technical boxer who studied Braddock's boxing style, and when they met in the ring on July 18, 1929, The Phantom had a strategy: he spent the fight artfully avoiding Braddock's powerhouse right hand. Braddock spent much of the rest of the fight chasing the elusive Loughran around the ring, stumbling and tripping as he went. Consequently, Braddock was unable to land enough clean, hard shots to secure a victory. After 15 rounds, Braddock lost his bid for the Light Heavyweight Title in a unanimous decision. He was demoralized, and thus began his decline in the heavyweight ranks. His record stood at 35-6 (21 KOs), and six draws.

Despite his loss to the "Phantom," the year 1930 began well for Jimmy Braddock with his marriage to his sweetheart Mae Fox on January 26. But Braddock was about to be knocked down again, this time by a force outside of the ring—one over which he had no control. What was to become labeled by historians as the Great Depression had begun with the stock market crash on October 29, 1929, known as "Black Tuesday." Braddock had accumulated some $20,000 in savings from his fight purses, which he had on deposit with the Bank of the United States. When the Bank of the United States went under on December 11, 1930 (and with no bank deposit insurance at the time), Braddock lost every cent he had in savings. Braddock took the loss in stride, reassuring himself that he was still young, and, that, as the top contender for the Light Heavyweight Championship, money was just around the corner. Indeed, most everyone in the Braddock camp would have agreed; there was much money to be made in the promising career of James J. Braddock.

But the Great Depression had devastating effects, and personal income, tax revenue, prices and profits plunged everywhere. Braddock's career would follow its downward spiral. In the ensuing years, from 1930-1933, Braddock was reduced to taking fights on short notice. Due in part to bad arthritis in his hands which caused them to be easily broken, he lost more often than he won. With every loss, his status suffered.

The boxer who was once regarded by *The Ring* magazine as "One of the World's Great Heavyweights," had been demoted to "journeyman" status, meaning that he was not regarded as a serious contender. Now Jimmy was booked only for fights that paid very little money. On March 1, 1933, Braddock suffered a loss against Philadelphia fighter Al Ettore, who had a 30-0 record with 13 KO's. However, more than the loss, the fight was painful for Braddock due to the humiliation he suffered. Unable to defend himself following a punch he threw that nearly shattered his right hand, Braddock was disqualified for "not trying." In the short four rounds of the discouraging contest, Braddock was jeered relentlessly as he attempted to duck Ettore's punches and pawed at him with his left hand. Meanwhile, the economy continued its descent, and Braddock became more and more desperate for money to support his family.

With his savings gone and his career in limbo, Braddock was forced to take on work outside the ring in order to bring in money and give his hands time to heal. He worked double shifts as a longshoreman on the waterfront of Hoboken, New Jersey, whenever possible, and picked up odd jobs as a bartender and laborer. But work was scarce during the Depression, and like many at that time, Braddock and his wife and three young children were living from hand to mouth. Braddock borrowed what he could, but his manager, Joe Gould, was having his own financial problems, and, with Braddock out of the ring, was forced to work as a door-to-door salesman. On September 25, 1933, things got even worse for the Braddock family when Braddock received a "no-contest" disqualification (for circumstances outside the fighters' control) when he broke his right hand in three places in a fight with Abe Feldman, who had brought an 18-1 record into the ring to challenge Braddock. With no income, the Braddocks' diet was reduced to potatoes, bread, and water, and there was no money for electricity or gas. Since they could not make the rent, the Braddocks were forced to relocate to a smaller, cramped apartment in the building where they lived through one of the coldest winters on record without electricity or heat. Finally, with nowhere to turn, Braddock was forced to file for $17-a-week government relief to support his family. As all of this unfolded, he was amazed to reflect that he had tumbled from top contender for the Heavyweight title, to tomato can (as perceived by some), to welfare recipient. Braddock felt completely and utterly defeated. Additionally, his boxing record had taken a pounding, and now stood at 46 wins (25 KOs), 25 losses (one by disqualification), 7 draws, and 2 "no contests."

By 1934, Braddock's hands had improved. As the bones healed, his spirits returned and, out of love for the sport and the necessity to care for his family, he eyed a return to the ring. Having outgrown the light heavyweight division's 175 pound limit, Braddock would now fight as a heavyweight at 180 pounds. Despite his overall lackluster performance the last time he had fought, Gould never gave up on Braddock. In June of 1934, due to last minute cancellation, Gould was able to secure a fight for Braddock against John "Corn" Griffin, a highly touted rising star who was expected to step over

Braddock easily. However, Braddock, realizing that this was his "shot," fought like a man possessed. As he had not fought for over nine months, his plan was to go for a quick knockout, before he had a chance to get winded. Despite being knocked down in the second round, Braddock reached back for everything he had and knocked out Griffin in the third round. He brought home his half of the $250 in earnings from the fight with pride and relief, as his family desperately needed the money. But even more importantly, he had won despite the odds against him. He felt good and strong, and thrilled to be back on the winning side of the boxing ledger. This fight would prove to be the turning point in his career.

Braddock's victory over Corn Griffin led to a fight on November 16, 1934, with John Henry Lewis. Lewis had an impressive record of 33-2, with 3 draws, and was aiming towards a title shot. Again, Braddock surprised the odds-makers and won. He received his half of the $750 in earnings which the fight paid and a big fight: a match-up on March 22, 1935, with top contender Art Lasky for a $4,100 payday to the Braddock camp. Despite Lasky's record of 37-4, with two draws, Braddock won a 15 round decision "easily" according to *The New York Times.* Braddock was "back," and working his way to the top. But the first thing he did with his winnings was pay back the $300 he had received from the welfare agency (and took himself off their rolls), along with paying off his back rent, electricity and other utilities. Only after his debts were settled and his family was properly provided for did Braddock devote funds to his training. Preparation would prove to be a necessity, for, in 1935, Jimmy became the #2 contender for the Heavyweight Title held by Max Baer.

Maximilian ("Max") Adelbert Baer was one of the hardest hitters in boxing history. And he was lethal—one of his opponents, Frankie Campbell, had died as a result of his devastating punches, and it was speculated that his heavy hands might have been a factor in the untimely death of 24-year-old Ernie Schaaf after Baer had knocked him senseless six months earlier. For Braddock's 1935 title shot with Baer, it was said that an ambulance had been discreetly hired to whisk Braddock away from the arena should he need to go to the hospital as a result of Baer's ring supremacy. Baer himself viewed Braddock as little more than an easy payday. As a playboy who paid little attention to training, Baer frequently joked around with the media and earned the nickname "Clown Prince of Boxing." The overconfident Baer had trained even less for this fight than usual, certain he would have an easy night of it from Braddock.

Braddock had his own strategy for Baer. He remembered the lesson he learned from Loughran years earlier, and, this time, he did his homework. Braddock went into the ring knowing that the key to victory was to stay away from Baer's sledgehammer right hand.

The odds were stacked 10-1 against Braddock, making him the biggest underdog in heavyweight championship history, but by the time the 192-pound Jimmy Braddock stepped in the ring on June 13, 1935, he was ready. For 15 rounds, the underrated Braddock evaded Baer's infamous right hook in a deliberate and quietly effective strategy. Gradually, Braddock piled up points with accurate punches. Braddock was also able to absorb any of the shots that Baer managed to connect, showing fortitude that perplexed and frustrated the heavy-hitting Baer. With his amazing mastery of the ring, fierce determination and perseverance, Braddock wore Baer down and won. David had beaten Goliath in one of the biggest upsets in boxing history. When the final bell rung, the crowd that night leapt to its feet and gazed in awe at a champion whose heart and soul had carried him to victory. At last, James J. Braddock was the Heavyweight Champion of the World. But he was also more than that: with this victory, Braddock became a beacon of hope for millions. Everyone reveled in celebration, not only for the against-all-odds accomplishment itself, but also for the hope it gave to the Depression-weary mentality of the country.

Braddock's status as a symbol of pride in the American consciousness was to be re-asserted two years later, when, at the age of 32, Braddock defended his title against rising star and future champion Joe Louis. On June 22, 1937, World Heavyweight Champion Jimmy Braddock stepped into the ring as a 5-1 underdog against the 23-year-old, highly touted Louis, who sported a record of 30-1 (25 KOs). In the first round, he excited the crowd when he floored Louis with an uppercut. But Braddock's arthritis prevented him from capitalizing on this opportunity, and Louis quickly took control of the fight. Round after round, Braddock held on, even after he lost a tooth which was knocked through his mouthpiece into his lip. Finally, after eight rounds, Braddock was knocked out. This was the only time in Braddock's 86-fight career that he was knocked out. By the end, Braddock's struggle was written on his face, where he received 23 stitches. Yet, Jimmy Braddock, who had fallen from the promising boxer and magazine cover story, to a journeyman booed in the ring, had risen to become revered in the American public eye. He received a prolonged ovation as he left the ring. The new champion Joe Louis, who would later successfully defend his title 25 times (21 by knockout) against some of the toughest heavyweights in the sport, would later describe Braddock as "the most courageous fighter I ever fought."

Even after his retirement, Braddock remained a fighter. Both he and Gould enlisted in the U.S. Army in 1942 and eventually become First Lieutenants. Braddock trained soldiers in hand-to-hand combat on the island of Saipan in the Pacific Theater. He returned home after the war and started a business, dealing in marine equipment. In later years, Braddock worked in the Operating Engineers Union 825, and helped build the Verrazano Bridge in New York City. It seemed there was nothing this man couldn't do. Sadly, he died of a heart attack in his sleep on November 29, 1974 at the age of 69. In *The New York Times*, Red Smith wrote, "If death came easily, it was the only thing in his life that did."[1]

Jimmy Braddock has continued to be a source of inspiration over the decades. A 2005 biographical film of his life entitled *Cinderella Man* was directed by Ron Howard and starred Russell Crowe as Braddock. It was Damon Runyon who dubbed this amiable, "never-say-die" Irish-American "The Cinderella Man," as his story of rugged blue-collar persistence, succeeding against all odds, gave the country hope during the Depression-era backdrop of the 30's. Had famed American author Horatio Alger been alive, he would have relished the opportunity to write about this rags-to-riches, unlikely boxing champion, whose determination was unflappable.

Few of us who did not go through the Great Depression can imagine how tough life was during that era. Jimmy Braddock was able to rise above his challenges and better himself by his boxing successes, gaining strength from any obstacle he faced. His persistence and determination, plus a strong will to overcome the obstacles constantly in front of him, helped him on the road to regain his dignity and become a world champion.

In everyday life, it is easy to allow the difficulties we encounter to keep us from achieving our goals. Obstacles come in many forms. They can be societal (racism), material (poverty), physical shortcomings, career setbacks, age, or lack of natural ability. No matter what path life takes, the ability to overcome obstacles, objections and disappointments is the key to success in any endeavor. Jimmy Braddock serves as an example to remind us that, no matter what setbacks present themselves, if we believe in ourselves, and can stand up when knocked down to fight on, we can overcome any challenge and rise above anything that life throws our way.

JOE CALZAGHE

Born: March 23, 1972, Hammersmith, England

Won WBO Super Middleweight Title: October 11, 1997 (defeated Chris Eubank)

Won IBF Super Middleweight Title: March 4, 2006 (defeated Jeff Lacy)

Won WBA and WBC Super Middleweight Titles: November 3, 2007 (defeated Mikkel Kessler)

Won *The Ring* magazine's Light Heavyweight Title: April 19, 2008 (defeated Bernard Hopkins)

Retired Undefeated: February 5, 2009

Record: 46 Wins, 0 Losses, 32 Knockouts

Boxing Handles: The Pride of Wales/The Italian Dragon

ROUND SEVEN

Winning Without Shortcuts

✦ Joe Calzaghe ✦

There are no shortcuts to any place worth going.

—Beverly Sills, opera singer

Joe Calzaghe's road to success was not quick and easy. After failing to qualify for the 1992 Olympics, he faced further setbacks throughout his career due to serious hand and wrist injuries. But he became a champion for all time—the hard way. Today, Calzaghe has permanently established himself in the winner's circle in boxing, with one of the best records in boxing history, retiring undefeated in 2009.

Winning in a boxing ring is always a challenge. Because of the inherent risks in the sport, one's fortunes can change at any moment. A champion boxer can be dethroned in an instant, with one punch, one misread move, one blink of an eye. Some boxers have to pay their dues the hard way, laboring in this tough sport over many years to get the recognition they deserve. For most, it never comes.

But for those with a hunger to win, like Calzaghe, the long road can pay off.

✦ ✦ ✦

IN 1992, AT the age of 17, fate stole the chance for Olympic gold from a young Welsh boxer. If it hadn't been for his determination in the years that followed, the world would have never learned his name: Joe Calzaghe.

Joe Calzaghe was born in Hammersmith, England, the son of an Italian father and a Welsh mother. His father, Enzo, originally from Sardinia, grew up in England and, after meeting Joe's mother, Jackie, decided to raise his family in Wales, which is where Joe grew up, along with his sisters, Sonia and Melissa.

By age 17, Joe Calzaghe, who had taken up boxing at the age of 10 to defend himself from school bullies, was eyeing Olympic Gold. With his father as trainer, Joe had won the Welsh schoolboy's title in 1985 at the age of 13 and a gold medal in the Gaelic Games, among others. With this track record, his father by his side, and remarkable drive and commitment, Joe seemed destined to represent his home country of Wales in the 1992 Barcelona Games. In 1989, with the Games only three years away, Calzaghe threw himself into an intense workout regimen. However, within his first year of training, Joe suffered a devastating injury to his right wrist. His doctor told him that the injury would leave him with a chronic, recurrent pain in his wrist, and, what was worse, that Calzaghe would probably never box again. Not only did it seem that his Olympic dream was stolen from him, but it seemed his real passion, boxing, had also been taken away.

But Joe would not give up—giving up would have been too easy.

After waiting a year for his wrist to heal, Joe started training again, using padded gloves in sparring sessions and wrapping his hand carefully. By this time the Barcelona games were only two years away and Calzaghe threw himself into a training regimen as serious and challenging as he could handle, even sparring with pros. In addition, he ran, hit the bags and the pads, and sparred with a sweat suit on (the added weight of the clothing made the workouts harder.) During these years of his Olympic training, his hard work paid off: he was runner-up in the Welsh championships in 1990, and fared well in a variety of European championships. By 1991, at age 19, Joe had reached the pinnacle of British amateur boxing. Again, it seemed his path was destined to lead to the Olympics. But, in a crushing blow, Joe was not nominated for the 1992 Olympic team on a technicality. Ian Irwin, who was head coach for the British Olympic squad that competed in Barcelona, used one word to describe the Welsh ABA's decision not to send Joe to the qualifiers. "Crazy."[1] However, the pain of this loss only increased when Joe watched his teammate Robin Reid earn a bronze medal and return from Barcelona a hero.

Being turned down for the 1992 Olympic team was a defining, character-shaping moment for Calzaghe. This disappointment resonated with him that the road to achieving his dreams would be long, difficult, and full of unexpected pitfalls and detours. Still, Joe pressed forward. In his autobiography, Joe wrote, about his drive to win, "People talk about hunger, but you have to feel it in your belly, that's the feeling you need to have."[2] In the case of Calzaghe, his Olympic disappointment fueled his hunger and drive to be champion.

Over the next year, Joe's hunger to make his mark in the sport, despite the disappointment of not being selected for the Olympic team, drove his strict training regimen. This desire to achieve fueled his next string of victories in the amateur circuit, during which he stopped every opponent he faced. In 1992 he won the ABA Title at Light Middleweight. Calzaghe fed the flames of his ambition with personal drive, staying patient and hungry, never losing sight of his goals. And there was an important principle that constantly guided him, one that was passed down to him by his father: don't cheat.

Training for boxing is a long, lonely endeavor. From hours to days, weeks and months to years, the boxer trains. His unforgiving regimen includes hitting the heavy bag and the speed bag, jumping rope, and working in the ring; and doing it all over and over again. The temptation to cut corners is always there. These are things a boxer does alone—even if he trains with someone else, his pain is his to bear. This can make for a strong temptation to cheat or cut corners. But Calzaghe knew he would ultimately be the person who would suffer. Joe's trainer and father, Enzo, says this of his son's commitment: "I'll be counting the rounds he's done on the bags and . . . I'll say, 'Ok, Joe, that's nine, so one more will do you.' But he'll turn round and tell me, 'That's not nine, it's eight.' Other fighters will cheat . . . Joe will never cheat."[3]

In September 1993, Joe signed with professional managers and promoters, and by June 1995, Joe had nine impressive victories under his belt; less than one year later, he was up to 19. But Calzaghe was a matchmaker's nightmare—it was nearly impossible to get opponents for him because he kept knocking out most everyone he faced. So, in 1996, Calzaghe made the switch to manager Frank Warren, who had managed former world champion Nigel Benn, also one of Great Britain's most famous and successful boxers.

On June 5, 1997, at age 25 with a record of 22-0, Calzaghe fought former WBO Super Middleweight Champion Chris Eubank for the WBO Super Middleweight title, recently vacated by Steve Collins. It was one of Joe's toughest fights, but he managed to defeat the experienced and highly touted Eubank and win by decision. Finally, Calzaghe had a world title belt to show for his hard work. He was now the WBO Super Middleweight Champion. Still, he longed for international recognition. By the year 2000, U.K. boxer Audley Harrison won the Olympic gold medal in Sydney, Australia, at Super Heavyweight in 2000, and signed a £ one million deal with the BBC. With every moment of glory for his countrymen, Joe felt the sting of regret for having missed Olympic glory and was tempted to believe that he would never be a superstar.

After a first round knockout of the previously undefeated (30–0) German, Mario Veit, on April 28, 2001, Joe was beginning to get some international recognition. He was now established as the top fighter in Britain, and he wanted to take on the biggest names in the sport, like Roy Jones, Jr., and Bernard

Hopkins. In the early part of the decade, these fights could not be arranged. For Joe it was simply a waiting game: he had to get "big enough" in terms of reputation to fight guys like Jones and Hopkins. Some athletes might have tried to gain a shortcut with performance-enhancing drugs. Not Calzaghe—again, no shortcuts. Calzaghe was yet to have his career defining fight, so that he could achieve true worldwide recognition and the money he deserved. Patiently, he waited it out, biding his time until he would face down an opponent big enough for his fight class—and tough enough to take on the undefeated Calzaghe. During this period, he disposed of a number of accomplished boxers from around the world, including Will McIntyre (United States), Charles Brewer (United States, former IBF Super Middleweight Champion), Miguel Angel Jimenez (United States), Tocker Pudwill (United States), Byron Mitchell (United States, former WBA Super Middleweight Champion), Mger Mkrtchian (Armenia), and Kabary Salem (United States/ Egypt), before a successful rematch with Mario Veit.

Still, Calzaghe longed for the chance to make a name for himself on the world stage of the sport. Although he was well known and highly regarded in the U.K., he was hardly a household name in the boxing world. As the undefeated World Boxing Organization (WBO) Super Middleweight Champion, Calzaghe had never fought outside of Europe—his opponents were largely from the U.K. and Europe, and he was little known outside of the British Isles. In 2004, he watched yet another countryman, Amir Khan, go to the Athens Olympics and return home to England with an Olympic silver medal and immediately become one of the biggest commodities in

British sport. Though Calzaghe had never had a chance to be an Olympian, he had now been a world champion for almost nine years. Finally, on March, 4, 2006, Calzaghe was to have a chance to make a name for himself: he was to fight American Jeff "Left Hook" Lacy, holder of the International Boxing Federation (IBF) Super Middleweight belt. In this 18th defense of his world title, Calzaghe's career defining opportunity had at last arrived.

Lacy was a former Olympian with an undefeated record of 21 wins, 17 of them by knockout, and was considered an excellent world-class fighter with great punching power. Lacy was frequently compared in stature and style to Mike Tyson and viewed by many to be one of the next great names in American boxing. The betting was heavily in favor of Lacy, and there were probably some American fans who wondered who exactly Lacy was going to fight that was worth the journey to Manchester, England. Lacy was defending his belt for the fifth time. Originally scheduled for November 2005, the fight had to be postponed after Calzaghe broke his left hand in a fight on September 10, 2005, with Kenyan Evans Ashira "The African Warrior." In the fourth round of the Ashira fight, Calzaghe broke the metacarpal bone in his left hand after he threw a left uppercut which somehow landed on the top of Ashira's head. It was a very bad injury, and from the moment of impact, Joe knew his hand was out of commission for the rest of the fight. Incredibly, he completed eight more rounds with a broken hand, and took the victory by a unanimous decision.

At this point, Joe Calzaghe had assembled an incredible record of 40 wins, no losses, with 31 knockouts. But by the time the original date for the Lacy fight had come, Calzaghe hadn't fully healed and the fight had to be postponed until March. Calzaghe's injury again fueled speculation that he simply wasn't fit to take on Lacy. For his part, the 29-year-old Lacy viewed 34-year-old Calzaghe as an over-the-hill boxer who would be easily beaten. But Calzaghe was used to injuries, and he was used to overcoming them. Though Calzaghe suffered serious injuries and had to nurse himself back to health, sometimes sitting out for months at a time, he always managed to somehow overcome these setbacks. Many people in his situation would have become disillusioned and discouraged. They would have quit during fights or given up the sport. Characteristically, Calzaghe fought on despite anything standing in his way.

By March 2006, crowds on both sides of the Atlantic were ready for a good fight. But the largely British crowd in Manchester's M.E.N. arena would have to wait several hours—until 2 a.m., in fact—so that the bout could be viewed live by the American television audiences. By the time Lacy and Calzaghe got to the ring, the crowd was nearly hysterical with anticipation. As the fighters disrobed, Lacy looked sculpted and powerful, practically a portrait of imminent victory. Calzaghe looked lean and hungry. Lacy's powerful but stocky build at 5'8" had resulted in a height advantage for the leaner, lankier Calzaghe at 5'11½". Both fighters were within the limit of the 168 pound Super Middleweight Division.

But anyone who had judged this fight based on first impressions was proved wrong from the get-go. Minutes into round one, what the audience saw was bearing witness to one of the most one sided title fights ever. Lacy had come into the fight with a false sense of security, misled by his own assumption that Calzaghe was not in his class professionally as a boxer. Instead, Calzaghe administered a master-class to the unsuspecting American. By the end of the third round, Lacy was bleeding from his nose and around both eyes, and his face was a mess. By the seventh, Lacy's legs looked unsteady. He kept taking punishment, until, by the twelfth round, Calzaghe decked him. Calzaghe had pitched an almost perfect game and won by a unanimous decision. Joe Calzaghe, the "Pride of Wales," was now 41-0, with 31 knockouts.

The effect that this had on Joe Calzaghe was to give him instant credibility on the world boxing stage and help him leverage himself to take on the fights that he had been scrambling for, and propel his career into superstardom. His time had come! He was heralded by the press as one of the very best in British boxing history. Never mind that he missed the Olympics, or that he had to endure eighteen title defenses before he got his big break. His moment came with Jeff Lacy—he seized it and now he was poised for the future in a big way. And he had made it look easy with Lacy. Now all kinds of possibilities would open up for him. From this point forward, he decided that he had set a standard in the Lacy fight that he wanted for the rest of his career.

Following impressive wins over Sakio Bika (Cameroon) and Peter Manfredo (United States) in 2006 and 2007, Joe was ready to take on Mikkel Kessler, the Danish fighter who held the WBA and WBC Super Middleweight Titles, and was also undefeated at 39-0 with 29 knockouts. In this highly anticipated match-up on November 3, 2007, of two undefeated fighters with near identical records, Kessler fought hard but Joe was too strong, and the unanimous decision over Kessler now meant Joe held four Super Middleweight Title belts.

This led him to the road he had wanted to travel all along—finally a match up with boxing great Bernard Hopkins (then 48 wins, 4 losses, 34 knockouts), who held *The Ring* Light Heavyweight Title, and was considered one of the smartest and craftiest fighters in the business. By getting this fight, which was held on April 19, 2008, in Las Vegas (his first time to fight in the U.S., and outside of Europe), Calzaghe officially arrived on the world boxing scene, and symbolically picked up the journey which he had been robbed of when he failed to qualify for the Olympics two decades earlier. Winning a split decision win over Hopkins, his perfect record was advanced to 45 wins, 0 losses, 32 knockouts, and he had successfully moved up to the light heavyweight division and become a champion overnight.

Calzaghe had come full circle when a match was arranged on November 8, 2008, with former Olympic medalist Roy Jones, Jr. (then 52 wins, 4 losses, 38 knockouts), at Madison Square Garden in New York City. A former world champion in four different weight classes and previously considered as one of the best pound-for-pound fighters in the world, Jones' star had faded somewhat in recent years following two big losses (to Antonio Tarver and Glen Johnson) but the Jones-Calzaghe fight still received much media attention. After Jones knocked Calzaghe down in the first round, Joe proved to be much too fast for the 39-year-old Jones, and he coasted to an easy unanimous victory.

On February 5, 2009, Joe Calzaghe retired, arguably the best British boxer of his era. As Joe himself wrote, "Nothing has ever been handed to me on a plate and I believe that's the reason I've been successful for so long."[4] He has claimed a special place in the record books, with 46 wins and no losses, with 32 knockouts. His career hearkens back to that of Rocky Marciano, whose record of 49-0 with 43 knockouts remains unsurpassed but inevitable comparisons are made. It must be said that anyone who can be realistically and factually compared to Marciano must go down in the record books as one of the best of all time. And like Rocky, he let nothing stand in his way until he reached the top of the sport in a journey that lasted 17 years as a professional boxer.

Joe Calzaghe's long journey to the pinnacle of boxing is testament to the fact that determination, focus and a sheer will to win are the best combination of all for success at anything. He proved without question that tenacity and steadiness of purpose can win in the end, and that sometimes the good guys do, too.

Frequently in business, politics, and all walks of life, there is much competition and many stumbling blocks that keep people from gaining rapid success and recognition. Though some people seem fortunate enough to vault up the corporate ladder, the slow and steady route can work as well. If one keeps improving and taking advantage of opportunities as they present themselves, success can be even more rewarding when it finally appears. Furthermore, success achieved in this way comes with unquestioned credibility, which elevates someone even further in the eyes of their peers, competitors, and critics. There is no better example of winning through tenacious resolve in any endeavor than Joe Calzaghe.

Obstacles don't have to stop you. If you run into a wall, don't turn around and give up. Figure out how to climb it, go through it, or work around it.

—Michael Jordan, basketball great

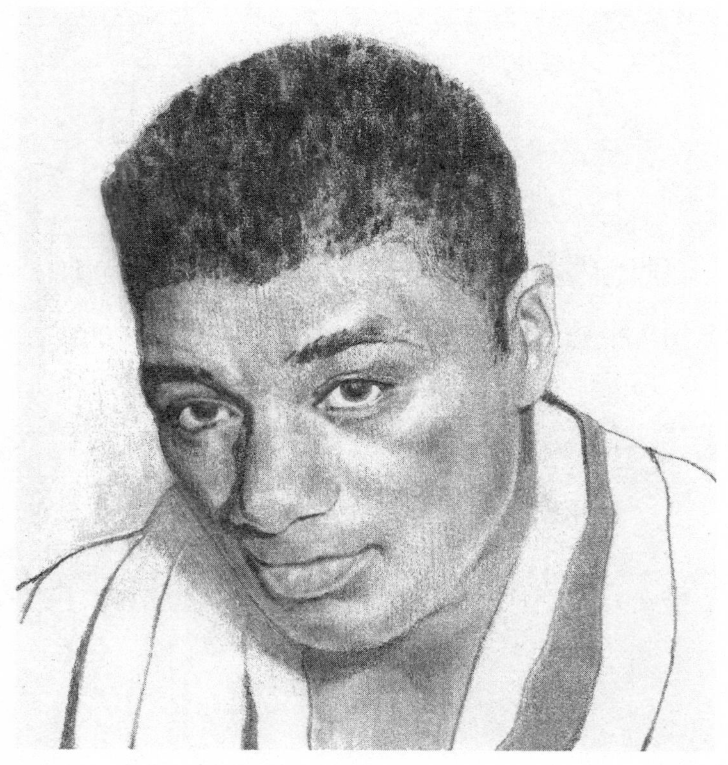

FLOYD PATTERSON

Born: January 4, 1935, Waco, North Carolina
Died: May 11, 2006, New Paltz, New York
Won vacant World Heavyweight Title: November 30, 1956 (defeated Archie Moore)
Lost World Heavyweight Title: June 26, 1959 (Ingemar Johansson)
Regained World Heavyweight Title: June 20, 1960 (defeated Ingemar Johansson)
Lost World Heavyweight Title: September 25, 1962
Record: 55 wins, 8 losses, 1 draw, 40 knockouts
Boxing Handle: The Gentleman of Boxing

ROUND EIGHT

Making Fear Your Friend

✦ Floyd Patterson ✦

Fear was absolutely necessary. Without it, I would have been scared to death.

—Floyd Patterson

By applying the lessons he learned from the great trainer, Cus D'Amato, Floyd Patterson overcame paranoia, shyness, and, ultimately, fear. Cus, one of boxing's foremost authorities on the subject of fear, helped Patterson, who was naturally "afraid of his shadow," use fear as a motivator to sharpen his game, train to his maximum potential, and win fight after fight.

All boxers experience fear. Indeed, in a sport that can cause great physical harm and even death, there is much to fear—including loss and humiliation. But, if harnessed correctly, fear can push boxers to train harder, prepare more thoroughly, and perform at a higher level than they would ordinarily. Fear, if overcome through intense mental and physical preparation, can enhance the possibility of success.

Floyd Patterson is a shining example of someone who successfully dealt with fear, learned how to use it to his advantage, and, ultimately, became Heavyweight Champion of the World—not once, but twice.

✦ ✦ ✦

FLOYD PATTERSON WASN'T really cut out to be a fighter. Nearly crippled by shyness as a boy, he was plagued by self-doubt as a fighter. Mild mannered and polite, Patterson was a "nice guy" inside the ring, in spite of its brutality; he would help his opponents off the floor and retrieve their mouthpieces after he knocked them out of their mouths. Yet Patterson was one of the most skilled fighters in the ring, and his achievements were remarkable. When all was said and done, he backed down from no one.

Floyd Patterson was born on January 4, 1935, in a cabin in North Carolina, the third of eleven children. Not long after Patterson's birth, the Patterson family moved to Brooklyn, New York, to escape the poverty of North Carolina and, hopefully, find work for Patterson's father, Thomas. Over the years, Thomas worked wherever and at whatever he could find, including as a contractor, longshoreman, sanitation worker and fishmonger. Yet his earnings never seemed to be enough to put food on the table, and the family struggled with poverty during Floyd's formative years.

The family was constantly on the move, so young Floyd missed school often, and had a difficult time making and keeping friends. At age 11, he could not read or write. He was so extremely shy that he would not speak to anyone and, even as a boy, Floyd suffered from extremely low self-esteem; once, he pointed to himself in a photograph of him and his brothers at the Bronx Zoo and told his mother, "I don't like that boy." As he grew, the future Heavyweight Champ had to wear his brothers' hand-me-downs. His sense of shame was acute.

In his autobiography, *Victory Over Myself,* he recalled, "I hated laughter because it seemed no matter what I did, everybody was always laughing at me. They'd laugh at the dirt on my face and the torn, shabby, over-sized clothes I wore, and the way I couldn't read or write or answer a question in school or even talk to somebody when they talked to me. It got so that I wouldn't look anybody in the face or want them to look at me." Ashamed of his appearance, Patterson avoided others by sneaking into any out-of-the-way place he could find, including dark hiding places, like cellars, subways, alleyways, and, if he could sneak in, movie theaters. Wrote Floyd, "I'd run and hide . . . I got to like the darkness. There was safety in the darkness for me."[1]

Eventually, Patterson began stealing to pass the time and in an effort to help his family with extra income. On occasion, Floyd stole enough to surprise his mother with a dress or other gifts he knew she couldn't otherwise afford. Soon, Patterson was stealing and getting caught so often that he had frequent court appearances. At this point, the future for young Floyd looked anything but bright; frustrated, Floyd's mother sent her son off to Wiltwyck School for Boys, a reform school in upstate New York. There, Patterson's teachers provided the attention and encouragement Patterson needed, and he soon learned to read. He also put on boxing gloves for the first time, and won all three bouts in which he participated. Still, although he learned how to smile and made a few friends, his basic fears and low self-esteem continued to dog him.

After almost two years at Wiltwyck, Patterson returned home. He attended special public and vocational schools for a while but dropped out to support his family. It was after he quit school, at the age of 14, that Patterson's life took a fateful turn.

One day, he accompanied his older brothers to the Gramercy Gym on the Lower East Side of Manhattan. Although the Gramercy Gym was somewhat run-down, it was owned and operated by the legendary Constantine ("Cus") D'Amato, considered one of the most creative trainers ever. Almost immediately after Patterson stepped in the ring, D'Amato recognized Patterson's talent and potential.

Any story of Floyd Patterson is closely aligned with the training methods and managerial brilliance of Cus D'Amato, who was a skilled, committed trainer and would also become Patterson's mentor. D'Amato would later successfully train Jose Torres and Mike Tyson. Considered one of boxing's foremost authorities on the subject of fear, Cus's training methods were centered around overcoming fear and using it as an asset in boxing. According to D'Amato, "Fear is natural, it is normal. Fear is your friend . . . Without fear, we would not survive."

Central to D'Amato's teaching methods was the principle that, "fear is an asset to a fighter. It makes him move faster, be quicker and more alert."[2] He understood the mindset of a fighter when he added, ". . . as the fighter walks toward the ring, his feet want to walk in the opposite direction. He's asking himself how he got into this mess. He climbs the stairs into the ring, and it's like going to the guillotine. Maybe he looks at the other fighter, and sees by the way he's loosening up that his opponent is experienced, strong, very confident. Then when the opponent takes off his robe, he's got big bulging muscles. What the fighter has to realize is that he's got exactly the same effect on his opponent, only he doesn't know it. And when the bell rings, instead of facing a monster built up by the imagination, he's simply up against another fighter."[3] D'Amato helped Patterson move past his fears by making him realize that his opponents experienced the same emotions of fear that he did, and that he would overcome his fears with more confidence in his own abilities which he would gain by more intense preparation in advance of a fight.

D'Amato also instructed Patterson on a boxing style he used for all of his champions, called "peek-a-boo." This is a unique boxing technique which positions the hands in front of the face with the fists at nose/eye level, as opposed to the more traditional style where the hands are at chin level, with the left hand about twelve inches in front of the chin and the right beside the chin (for a right handed fighter). Other unique features of the peek-a-boo style include elbows tucked in to protect the ribs, side to side head movements, and bobbing and weaving that culminate in blind-siding an opponent with surprise punches.

One year after his arrival at D'Amato's gym, in 1950, Floyd began boxing as an amateur and started his meteoric rise to stardom. With his soulful, sad eyes and almost silent demeanor, he appeared to be anything but a fighter when not in the ring. However, Patterson had learned to use his fears as fuel towards his opponents through D'Amato's teachings, and, on top of that, his peek-a-boo boxing technique served him well. His confidence grew, and his careful mental, physical, and psychological preparation for his fights sharpened his skills. In the ring, he had the look of an animal ready to unleash. As D'Amato described it, Floyd "fought from a crouch, and when he saw an opening, he would leap in with long punches. He threw punches fast and could land several in combination before his opponent could recover from the first."[4] By 1951, Patterson proved he had overcome his fears enough to earn the New York Golden Gloves as a middleweight. He was only 16. Yet Patterson had the skills to win, and, after sweeping the Eastern and Inter-city titles in 1952, he went on to win the gold medal in the Olympic Games in Helsinki at the age of 17. With five knockouts in five bouts as a middleweight, he pummeled his opponents easily and brought home a gold medal.

It seemed nothing could stop Patterson, who turned professional in 1952, at the age of 17. He won his first 13 professional fights easily, a feat due in part to D'Amato's artful management; D'Amato knew Patterson's fears well, and he carefully steered Patterson away from potential losses, sensing that defeat would be too much for Patterson. In fact, D'Amato's instincts were right on. When, two years into his professional career, Floyd lost in a close bout to former World Light-Heavyweight Champion Joey Maxim, in 1954, Patterson responded with behavior that was to become his automatic response to defeat: he locked himself away in his apartment. After being coaxed back to work by D'Amato, Patterson accumulated a string of victories, first as a light heavyweight then as a heavyweight. Before he knew it, in 1956 Patterson was next in line to challenge for the World Heavyweight Title recently vacated by newly retired Rocky Marciano.

On November 30, 1956, Patterson faced Light Heavyweight Champion Archie Moore for the World Heavyweight Championship. Patterson dominated in the ring, knocking Moore out in five rounds. Patterson was now the World Heavyweight Champion, and he also made history—just two months shy of his 22nd birthday, he became the youngest World Heavyweight Champion ever, in addition to being the first Olympic gold medalist to win a World Heavyweight Title.

Of Patterson's career as World Heavyweight Champ, his three epic battles against Ingemar Johansson, the European Heavyweight Champion from Sweden deserve special mention. Bigger and heavier than Patterson, Johansson had fought as a heavyweight in the Olympics in Helsinki, but had been disqualified in the finals for not trying, due to his opponent's punching power. Patterson lost the World Heavyweight Title to Johansson in 1959, after being knocked down seven times during the final round by Johansson's heavy right hand which he had labeled "The Hammer of Thor." Again, Patterson shut himself away in shame and refused all visitors. He was able to avenge this loss and regain the World Heavyweight Title with two subsequent victories over Johansson—on June 20, 1960, with a fifth round knockout, and then with a sixth round knockout on March 13, 1961. Still, although he had shown his might over Johansson, Patterson had still not entirely come to terms with his greatest challenger: fear.

Patterson would have the chance to demonstrate his mastery over fear one year later, when he had the opportunity to fight Charles "Sonny" Liston, although D'Amato, acting from concern that Patterson might lose, strongly recommended that Patterson turn down the fight. The public wanted the match and Patterson had his share of followers, including President John F. Kennedy who was a supporter of Patterson's, but cautioned him about fighting Liston. On his own merit and following a visit to the White House with President Kennedy, Patterson decided to take on Liston. At the time, the "presumed" 30-year-old Liston was generally perceived to be invincible (Liston's true age was always a mystery, with estimates ranging up to four years apart). Patterson and Liston were one inch apart in height—Liston was 6'½", and Patterson 5'11½". However, at the peak of his career, Liston ranged in approximate weights from 214–218 pounds, and Patterson was considerably smaller, at his peak ranging in weight from approximately 182-192 pounds. However, in order to win, Patterson would have to overcome the challenge and fear of Liston's reputation long before he stepped in the ring.

Patterson and Liston met on September 25, 1962, at Comisky Park in Chicago. From the beginning, things did not go well for Patterson, who seemed almost paralyzed by the sight of the glowering, brawny Liston. In the next 126 seconds, Liston annihilated Patterson. Later that evening, an embarrassed Patterson donned dark glasses, a fake mustache and beard before leaving the stadium by back entrance. He took the first opportunity he could to leave the country, sequestering himself in a cheap hotel in Europe for several days before finally returning home.

But Patterson still had a chance to prove himself: there was a rematch clause in the contract with Liston. Given the beating he took in the first fight, few would have faulted Paterson for letting the rematch go. But Patterson insisted on a return bout. As he said, "If I stopped now, that would be running away. I did that when I was a kid. I've grown out of that."[5] Putting his fears in the background, Patterson faced down Liston for the second time on July 22, 1963. Unfortunately, this fight lasted only four seconds longer than their previous encounter, and Liston walked away the winner with another first round KO. Nevertheless, the courage Patterson had shown in agreeing to take on the mighty Liston a second time was remarkable.

For the next 10 years, Patterson fought as a contender, as he was no longer champion. As a final testament to his ability to put his fears in the rear view mirror, Patterson twice fought Muhammad Ali, the man who had twice knocked out his nemesis Sonny Liston. Patterson was knocked out by Ali (in 12 rounds on November 22, 1965) and again on September 20, 1972 (in seven rounds). That same year, he retired and became a respected front man for the sport, active in the New York State Athletic Commission including serving three years as

Chairman. He also led a successful campaign to have the state mandate thumbless gloves to reduce eye injuries.

By any measure, Floyd Patterson fought the meanest, toughest men of his era, using fear as a motivator. During his career, Patterson was knocked down a lot, more than any previous heavyweight champion by some tallies. When questioned about this, he responded, "Yes, but I also got up more than anyone."[6] It is this remark that best summarizes the courage and resolve of this respected champion who refused to let fear stand in his way.

By looking fear straight in the eye and facing it head-on, Floyd Patterson overcame his personal doubts and fears and reached his goals, time and again, despite overwhelming odds, physical limitations and frustrating setbacks.

With life, it is much the same. Everyone experiences fear—fear of failure or inadequacies—in all endeavors. The parallels in career, education, politics, and any field are clear. Too often, people give up the task at hand, and let fear control them. However, by facing fears with courage and resolve, fear can in fact provide motivation, inspiration and energy, which can help us conquer any obstacle that stands in our way.

Fear is motivational. Fear produces intensity. And fear leads to success.

What matters most is how you walk
through the fire.

—Charles Bukowski, German American
poet and writer

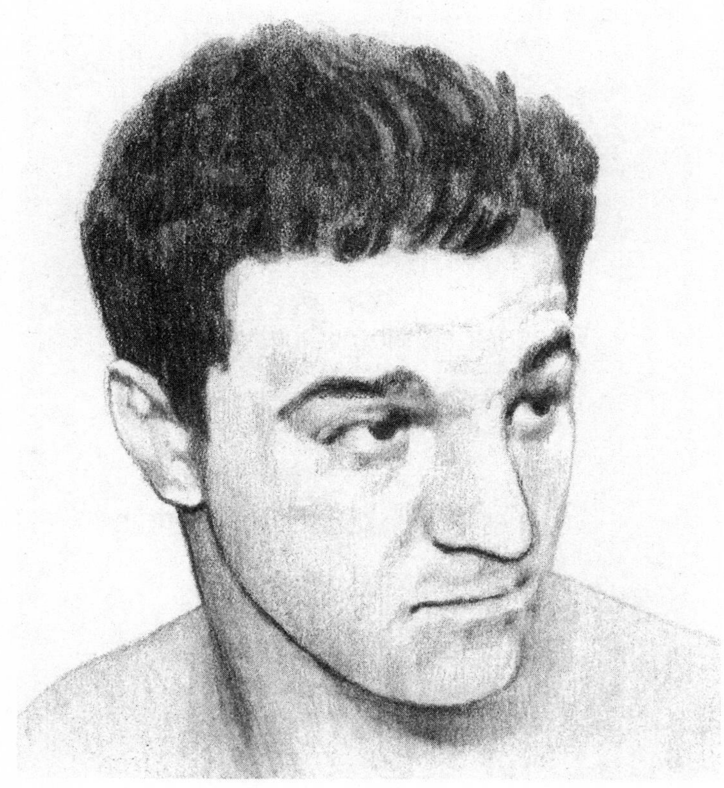

ROCKY MARCIANO

Born: September 1, 1923, Brockton, Massachusetts

Died: August 31, 1969, near Newton, Iowa

Won World Heavyweight Title: September 23, 1952 (defeated Jersey Joe Walcott)

Retired: As Undefeated Champion, April 27, 1956

Record: 49 wins, 0 losses, 43 knockouts

Boxing Handle: The Brockton Blockbuster, a.k.a. "The Rock"

Overcoming Pain

✦ Rocky Marciano ✦

> Pain is temporary. It may last a minute, or an hour, or a day, or a year, but eventually it will subside and something else will take its place. If I quit, however, it lasts forever.
>
> —Lance Armstrong, Famed Road Racing Cyclist

Rocky Marciano brought more heart into the ring than any fighter in the history of the sport. A relatively small man for a heavyweight, he became as indestructible as any fighter in ring memory. The only heavyweight king in history to win every contest as a professional boxer, the vast majority by knockout, he just kept on winning and reached legendary status in the sport. Yet it was his willingness to endure as much punishment as necessary to win that truly set him apart. He seemed impervious to pain, as he was always ready to take multiple punches to land one, never letting anything stand in his way.

Boxing is known as the "pain business." Because of its intense physical contact and adversarial nature, pain is an essential ingredient of the sport. How a boxer deals with pain can make the difference between winning and losing, fighting or giving up, dignity over humiliation.

Rocky Marciano's ability to overcome pain in the ring helped him achieve a record in the heavyweight division which has not been matched before or since.

Born Rocco Francis Marchegiano to Italian immigrants Pierino Marchegiano and Pasqualina Picciuto, Rocky tipped the scales at 12 pounds on the day of his birth, September 1, 1923. He had his first bout at 18 months, when he contracted pneumonia. Though he nearly died, Rocky pulled through, impressing doctors with his strong constitution.

The eldest of six, Rocky was raised during the Depression in Brockton, Massachusetts, where the family lived frugally on Pierino's income from the shoe factory. Stocky and muscular as a boy, Rocky got his start in boxing by punching a stuffed mail bag that hung from a tree in his backyard as a heavy bag. Around the neighborhood, he became respected in playground altercations and was known as the "really tough Italian kid." Yet although he admired the great boxer, "Brown Bomber" Joe Louis, young Rocky chose baseball and football over boxing. Even as a boy, Rocky trained tenaciously: to prep for baseball, Rocky would hit and chase down baseballs to the point of exhaustion. Then he would go home and do chin-ups and lift homemade weights until he was totally spent.

At age 15 during his sophomore year at Brockton High School, a school well-known for its football program, Rocky played varsity center, and the following spring, earned a spot as catcher on the varsity baseball team. After he was cut from the high school baseball team for playing on two teams at once (he also played in a church league), Rocky lost interest in school and dropped out before his junior year. Almost right away, Rocky looked for work and landed a job as a "chute man" on a Brockton Ice and Coal delivery truck, and then in the shoe factory where his father worked, before being drafted into the army in 1943 at age 20.

Rocky was sent away to England and then brought back to Fort Lewis, Washington, to await orders. It was during his tour of duty in England that Rocky started throwing punches again. One night in England, he flattened a big Australian soldier who was giving him and his buddies a hard time in a pub. Then, at Fort Lewis, Rocky took up boxing out of boredom and as a way to avoid "KP," or duty in the kitchen. He displayed natural ability, and in April of 1946, on a two-week furlough to Brockton where he boasted of his boxing skills, he was matched up against a former Golden Gloves Heavyweight Champion in a local fight. Although Rocky lost the bout, he was encouraged by praise he received on his overall performance.

After being honorably discharged from the army that summer, Rocky continued to fight as an amateur. By this time, he had given up smoking and drinking, began dieting, and increased his exercise regimen. His efforts paid off, and he won a rogue professional fight on March 17, 1947, where he fought under the name of "Rocky Mack."

Still, Rocky only became fully committed to boxing when

his dream of a career in baseball fell through. Although he made it to tryouts as a catcher with the Chicago Cubs, he was rejected because he couldn't accurately throw the ball from home plate to second base. It appeared that Rocky would have to stick to throwing punches.

Resigned to the fact that his only hope of a professional sports career would be in boxing, Rocky returned to the amateur circuit. He ended his amateur stint with a record of eight wins and four losses in 12 bouts (plus the one professional win already on his record) and officially turned pro on July 12, 1948. Although no one could have known it at the time, the four amateur losses Rocky had behind him were the only ones he would ever experience; from the moment he turned pro to the day he retired, Rocky would never experience another loss in the boxing ring.

Although his amateur record was impressive and Rocky's first official fight as a pro ended in victory with a first round TKO on July 12, 1948, Rocky's lack of training was obvious. Furthermore, he had more than a few strikes against him: not only was Rocky old for someone at the start of a professional career (almost 25), but he had a short reach and was slow on his feet. He lacked finesse in the ring and was also small for a heavyweight. At just under 5'10½" and weighing-in at only 185 pounds, Rocky wasn't exactly an imposing figure. He needed help if he was going to make it.

Through a friend, Rocky found a trainer in New York City named Charley Goldman. Goldman turned out to be the perfect match for Rocky. Although Goldman was impressed with Rocky's raw power and sheer guts, it was clear there was a lot of work to be done. Though scrappy and determined, Marciano struggled with traditional form and stance. Describing the first time he saw Rocky in the ring, Goldman recalled, "Marciano was so awkward we just stood there and laughed. He didn't stand right, he didn't throw a punch right. He didn't do anything right."[1]

Under Goldman's tutelage, Rocky hunkered down to hone his skills, beginning what was to be a determined and all-consuming journey to become a champion. Goldman modified Rocky's wade-in, take-no-prisoners, swarming style by teaching Rocky how to cut off the ring so he could get close enough to his opponent to cause real damage. To make his punches even more potent, Goldman also put Rocky on a training regimen where he would throw punches, non-stop. This became the chief, guiding principle of Rocky's offense: volume, volume, volume. However, Goldman could not prevent Rocky from the damage he took along the way due to his small size and the straight ahead nature of his attack. Despite the emphasis Goldman had placed on volume of punches, Rocky was frequently known to receive three to four punches with the hope of being able to deliver one. Consequently, much of the blood seen in the ring during a tough contest was Rocky's—evidence of the dues he had to pay before he could close the distance and inflict his devastating right hand, which became known as the "Suzie-Q."

After taking on the name Marciano at the suggestion of his handlers (who deemed Marchegiano too hard to pronounce), Rocky began a career that, even by today's standards, was relentlessly fast-paced. The rate at which Rocky took on all challengers was incredible: 11 fights in 1948, 13 in 1949, and six in 1950. Most fights ended in knockouts, many in the early rounds. Rocky's handlers made certain that nothing interrupted his momentum, even trying to dissuade him from marrying Barbara Cousens, the daughter of a Brockton Police Department patrolman, on New Year's Eve, 1950. But, really, they didn't have to worry; no one pushed Rocky harder than Rocky himself.

Rocky would take months to prepare for a fight, often secluding himself from his family and friends so he could focus completely on the impending bout. As Joyce Carol Oates describes it in *On Boxing*, "During the last 10 days before a fight he would see no mail, take no telephone calls, meet no new acquaintances. During the week before the fight he would not shake hands. Or go for a ride in a car . . . For all that was not 'the fight' had to be excluded from consciousness."[2] In his isolation, with the outside world left behind, Rocky restructured his thoughts, his mindset. Back in the ring, his monk-like asceticism gave him total focus and absolute presence of mind despite the desperation of the moment. The key to Rocky's ability to absorb pain was undoubtedly the result of a training regimen unparalleled in the sport, and his intense concentration.

Victory after victory was chalked up by the unstoppable Marciano, who, it seemed, would walk through fire if required in order to reach his goal. Constantly advancing, he took on any barrage of jolting, bone-crushing blows. The crowds loved Rocky, for his constant forward motion reassured them that they were getting their money's worth with every second he was in the ring. Between fights, Rocky's determination to make himself champion manifested itself through endless workouts, attacking his weaknesses, among them his small size and a weak left hand. His focus paid off, and at age 28, with a record of 37-0 and 32 KO's under his belt, the 184 pound Marciano was given the chance to fight his childhood hero, former Heavyweight Champion, Joe Louis.

But this fight would prove to be painful in a way that even Rocky couldn't fully prepare for. At the time, Louis, 38, was at the end of his career and was only staying in the ring to earn money to pay off back taxes. Rocky, aware that Louis was well past his prime, did not want to fight the "Brown Bomber," for whom he had so much admiration and respect. But if he wanted a shot at a title, Rocky would have to do it. With no choice but to fight, Rocky begin preparing for the October bout in which Louis was slightly favored to win.

By the date of the fight, October 26, 1951, Rocky was ready, but reluctant. In his dressing room that night, he said, "This is the last guy on earth I want to fight."[3] But Rocky had a job to do, and the fight did not have to go the distance for Rocky to overwhelm Louis, whose skills had clearly diminished over the past few years. In the eighth round, Louis was floored with several huge hooks and, moments later, ended his career from the ring apron. A distraught Rocky had tears in his eyes as he left the ring. Later, Rocky paid a visit to Louis's dressing room in a display of humility for the great former champ. Rocky was now 38-0, with 33 knockouts and well on the way to becoming world champ. In the meantime, he had obtained financial security and could finally realize a lifelong dream of telling his father he could retire from the shoe factory.

One year after his fight with Louis, Marciano would enter the ring for his signature fight, the one that would live forever in the annals of the sport. On September 23, 1952, Rocky faced Heavyweight Champion "Jersey Joe" Walcott for the title. Walcott, 38, had mastered the ability to throw his opponents off balance by sliding just out of reach. Walcott figured that Rocky would never be able to lay a hand on him.

When the time came to step into the ring, it seemed Walcott had guessed right; within the first 40 seconds, Walcott dumped Marciano on the canvas. This was the first time in his career that anyone had knocked Rocky down. Rocky made it back on his feet by the count of three, but Walcott's punch let Rocky know he was in for long night. Over the next 12 rounds, the crowd witnessed a seesaw battle. During the middle rounds, Rocky took a fearful beating and Walcott seemed to have the momentum to win. But Rocky was also wearing down Jersey Joe with his heavy sledgehammer pounding to his body and arms. As the championship rounds came into view, Walcott was ultimately judged to have gotten the better of it: he was ahead on all three judges' cards.

By round 13, Marciano was battered, bruised and bleeding, and his vision was compromised. But then Rocky's moment came. Both boxers were going for the knockout, when Walcott attempted to throw a left hook although his arms, hindered by the beating from Rocky, failed him. Seeing an opportunity, Rocky Marciano threw the punch of a lifetime and unleashed his Susie-Q. Traveling just a few inches, it was a short, show-stopping, power punch that connected squarely on Walcott's chin. Almost in slow motion, Walcott collapsed against the ropes, reaching instinctively for the middle rope as he fell first on one knee, and then slowly toppled forward. He landed on his forehead and stayed down, exhausted and immobile, while the referee finished his count. A photograph taken that night, showing the distortions to Walcott's face at the moment of impact of Marciano's right hand, is still considered one of the most revealing depictions of the damage that can be inflicted on the human face by a well-placed punch, with his features distorted into an ugly caricature. Rocky Marciano, the shoemaker's son from Brockton, was now Heavyweight Champion of the World. His record was glorious: 43-0, with 38 knockouts.

As brutal as Rocky's battle against Jersey Joe had been, more punishment was to come. In the next year, two of Rocky's most painful battles took place months apart, both against another former champion, Ezzard Charles "The Cincinnati Cobra" in Yankee Stadium, New York. The first, on June 17, 1954, demonstrated that the 32-year-old Charles, a clever boxer and solid puncher, was more than a match for Rocky. Their clash was one of the most grueling ever for the Heavyweight Championship, a savage, tortuous brawl which left blood streaming out of a gash above Rocky's left eye. Yet Rocky rallied toward the end of the fight, using his youth and stamina to stage a spectacular finish and a victory in a close, 15-round decision. Charles was the only man to ever last 15 rounds with Rocky, and, three months later, he would come at Rocky with even more fortitude and power. And, during that second meeting, even more blood was shed and pain inflicted.

On September 17, 1954, Rocky and Charles were at it again. In the sixth round, Charles split open the left nostril in Marciano's nose with a horrible vertical gash. Rocky's nose was grotesquely severed and the bleeding was so bad that, one round later, Goldman warned Rocky that the fight might have to be stopped. Still, despite this injury and a cut in the corner of his left eye, Rocky reached back for everything he had in the eighth round and closed the show by knocking Charles out with a mere 24 seconds remaining.

Marciano was victorious in his last title bout one year later, leaving him an incredible career record of 49-0, with 43 KO's. On April 27, 1956, Rocky retired from the ring, the only Heavyweight Champion to hang up his gloves with an undefeated record. Despite repeated offers, he refused to make a comeback.

In his post-fight years, Rocky enjoyed celebrity status, sharing honors with Joe DiMaggio as one of the most beloved athletes in the Italian-American community. Still, Rocky avoided getting too caught up in his successes and remained shy and soft-spoken, a "regular guy." He worked as a boxing commentator and referee for a few years. Then, on August 31, 1969, one day before his 46th birthday, Rocky traveled from Chicago to Des Moines on a small 3-passenger jet, to watch a young fighter. Bad weather set in over Iowa, and, in an attempted emergency landing, the plane collided with a tree in a cornfield. All three passengers died instantly.

Rocky was known for saying "great athletes find a way to win," and proved this to everyone by never losing a fight. Tenacious, relentless and determined, Rocky used intense ring preparation and concentration to create a "zone" for himself, where he could absorb whatever pain and punishment necessary to secure victory after victory over some of the best fighters in the business. Ignoring personal discomfort, Marciano had the ability to relentlessly rise above the crisis of the moment, never backing off, no matter the costs, or the pain. He was of one piece; he was his own man. He was a true champion, for any era.

✦ ✦ ✦

An important reason Rocky Marciano was able to become a champion was because of his ability to suppress pain, overlook discomfort, and remain focused on the task at hand in order to achieve his goals. Like any other obstacle, pain in boxing is an impediment to a goal, but a more intense and threatening component, due to the nature of the sport and the fact that one suffers in solitude. Rocky was able to apply unwavering concentration at all times and overcome pain throughout his career.

In life, who amongst us doesn't feel pain, not only pain from physical injury, but emotional pain? How one handles pain shapes one's character, and, ultimately, his or her ability to succeed.

We should all learn from Rocky Marciano whose presence of mind and intense concentration—even when he was subjected to great physical pain —not only kept him moving forward, but helped him win . . . again, and again, and again.

BERNARD HOPKINS

Born: January 15, 1965, Philadelphia, Pennsylvania

Won vacant IBF Middleweight Title: April 29, 1995 (defeated Segundo Mercado)

Won WBC Middleweight Title: April 14, 2001 (defeated Keith Holmes)

Won WBA Middleweight Title: September 29, 2001 (defeated Felix Trinidad)

Won WBO Middleweight Title: September 14, 2004 (defeated Oscar de la Hoya)

Lost Middleweight Titles: July 16, 2005 (Jermaine Taylor)

Won *The Ring* magazine's Light Heavyweight Title: June 10, 2006 (defeated Antonio Tarver)

Lost *The Ring* magazine's Light Heavyweight Title: April 19, 2008 (Joe Calzaghe)

Record 49 wins, 5 loses, 1 draw, 1 no-contest, 32 knockouts

Boxing Handle: The Executioner

ROUND TEN

Discipline and Preparation

✦ Bernard Hopkins ✦

> If I always appear prepared, it is because before entering an undertaking, I have meditated long and have foreseen what might occur. It is not genius that reveals to me suddenly and secretly what I should do in circumstances unexpected by others; it is thought and preparation.
>
> —Napoleon Bonaparte

In the world of boxing, Bernard Hopkins is known as a man who used the sport to turn his life around. He achieved success as a boxer through a rigorous training schedule, much determination and sacrifice, and a studious work ethic that included a continuous study of the sport and of the fight films of his opponents.

In boxing, success demands discipline and intense preparation. This means hour upon hour, day after day, of repetitive exercises—heavy bag, speed bag, jump rope, ring work, pushups, sit-ups, lifting weights, shadow boxing, sparring, working with the trainer on the mitts—over and over and over again. This rigorous training has to be balanced with diet and good personal habits. All of these disciplines have to be coupled with developing and maintaining a mindset that gives a fighter confidence in his/her ability to meet any challenge that presents itself.

In the case of Bernard Hopkins, discipline and preparation made all of the difference. These traits define him, and his success in the ring—they became his mantra.

✦ ✦ ✦

THE DETAILS OF Bernard Hopkins' background are similar to many boxers' life stories: a young man learns to fight in the city streets; later, he uses his abilities to make a living as a boxer, and, eventually, earn respect and credibility in the world of professional boxing. But unlike most, Bernard Hopkins achieved success and fame beyond his wildest dreams—due in large part to his unwavering discipline and commitment to intense preparation. The story of Bernard Hopkins is one of tragedy and, ultimately, triumph.

A Philadelphia native, Hopkins grew up in a housing project in one of the city's meanest neighborhoods, and became involved in crime and gang related activity at a young age. By age 13, he had been stabbed three times. When he was only 17, Hopkins was convicted of nine felonies resulting from "strong-arm robberies," (robbery where the perpetrator uses brute force to rob a victim rather than a weapon) and was sentenced to 18 years in the state penitentiary. Hopkins served just under 5 years in the Graterford State Penitentiary in Pennsylvania, regarded as one of the roughest prisons in the country. There, from 1984–1988, this fiercely independent, 6'½" future champion was confined to a small cell, which he shared with a cellmate. For 56 months of his life, Hopkins would be known as prisoner # Y4145. Yet, by the end of his time in prison, Hopkins would find himself, and build a new identity and a new life.

At Graterford, Hopkins devoted himself to turning his life around. He earned his high school diploma and converted to Islam. His dedicated approach to his faith helped him develop a focused, almost monastic approach to boxing, and he won the national penitentiary Middleweight Championship three times. Upon his release in 1988, Hopkins stayed on a straight and narrow path to personal betterment. Since his release, he has kept completely out of trouble, never even receiving a speeding ticket. He devoted himself to finding a job and a place to live in Philadelphia, and, after taking on some odd jobs, found steady work in a hotel. But he hadn't forgotten about boxing.

One day, Hopkins walked into Augie's Gym in Philadelphia. He had one thing on his mind: he was there to see Bouie Fisher, one of Philly's most highly-regarded trainers. Hopkins knew he was inexperienced, and also knew that, being older for someone beginning a career as a professional boxer, he was at a disadvantage. Still, Hopkins approached Bouie with determination. After Hopkins introduced himself, Fisher was less than impressed. He told Hopkins he saw many others come into the gym with the dream of turning pro—many who were much younger than Hopkins—and only a few of them made it. But Hopkins was insistent, and, although he was skeptical, Bouie agreed to work with Hopkins. It wasn't long before Hopkins set himself apart from the other boxers with his hard-working, never-quit mentality. Hopkins improved at lightning speed, and on October 11, 1988, he had his first professional fight—a four-rounder against a little known boxer. Hopkins lost by the decision of the judges. Disappointed, Hopkins retreated back to his day job at a hotel. Still, he kept up his boxing regimen. It was over a year until he fought again, but when he came back, his discipline and preparation paid off. In his February 22, 1990, bout, he defeated his opponent in four rounds.

After this taste of victory, Hopkins devoted himself entirely to boxing. For two years, he threw everything he had towards the sport, and his record showed it: he won 20 fights in a row, without a loss. Even more incredibly, 15 of these fights were by knockout, with 11 victories occurring in the first round. Suddenly, the boxing world was forced to sit up and pay attention to this steely-eyed, chiseled warrior who seemed to come out of nowhere, appearing in the ring and walking over his opponents with relative ease.

In 1993, Hopkins officially "announced" his arrival to the boxing world with a fight that was his first real opportunity for a world title, the vacant IBF World Middleweight crown. Hopkins was matched up against Roy Jones Jr. who was a much bigger name at the time. Jones was undefeated (21-0, with 20 knockouts), and had the prestige of an Olympic medal from the 1988 Olympics in Seoul. On May 22, 1993, Hopkins faced down the former Olympic champ, using everything he had and putting up a fierce fight. After 12 hard fought rounds, Jones was awarded a unanimous decision. But instead of giving up, Hopkins's disappointment fueled his efforts. He returned to what he knew best: work, practice, and discipline. For the next fight, he would be even better prepared.

One year later, Hopkins had another shot at a title. On December 17, 1994, Hopkins faced down Segundo Mercado for the vacant IBF World Middleweight Title, in Mercado's native Ecuador. Hopkins was floored twice, once in the fifth and once in the seventh, but still managed to gain a draw, with no winner or loser declared. Mercado remains the only man ever to knock down Hopkins in a professional bout. Although he didn't take the belt, Hopkins left the ring with more determination than ever. Again, he returned to his rigorous training routine, going back to his disciplined methods, trusting that his work would pay off. And, one year later, Hopkins had the chance at a re-match. On April 29, 1995, Hopkins dispatched Mercado in seven rounds and captured the IBF World Middleweight Title. But this was just the beginning: Hopkins was about to go down in history as the longest reigning World Middleweight Champion ever. For 10 long years, Hopkins would reign as World Middleweight Champ.

In 2001 when Hopkins entered a four-man competition organized by Don King to determine the undisputed World Middleweight Champion. Although the series was intended to be a coronation of King's fighter Felix Trinidad, it was Hopkins who stole the show and won the tournament by knocking out Trinidad in the twelfth round of the grand finale match of the series on September 29, 2001. With this win, Hopkins had truly arrived on the world stage he had been seeking.

His long road, full of sacrifice and tunnel-like focus, had paid off. He now held the IBF, WBC and WBA Middleweight Championship belts.

As he progressed on his journey, Hopkins acquired a unique style that was verbalized by Hall of Fame trainer Emanuel Steward when he described him as "an extremely intelligent fighter who is better at making adjustments as he goes along than anyone since Marvin Hagler . . . He can fight a technical fight, he can rough you up, whatever it takes. That's a gift few fighters have."[1] Hopkins has the ability to adapt to the style of any opponent and does everything well—slug, box, counter-punch or be slick. However, as his style developed, he often found his methods centered on wearing his fighters down over a number of rounds, rather than scoring an exciting win by knockout, which did not help his appeal at the box office. Consequently, he remained below that radar screen which was reserved for fighters considered more exciting to watch.

Along the way, Hopkins acquired a unique nickname—"The Executioner"—given to him by a fellow fighter who, watching him in the ring, commented that, with his penetrating eyes, taut facial features, tightly drawn lips and lithe body, he looked like an executioner. Hopkins would later make the most of that nickname by entering the ring masked with a big gold "X" across his face and in a red or black robe, looking much like the "grim reaper," complete with attendants draped in chains, ropes and hooded robes, carrying makeshift axes. Underneath his dramatic costume was Hopkins, with his stern expression and serious demeanor, carrying out the role in an intimidating and threatening manner. Even in a sport with much fanfare and showmanship, this ring entrance by "The Executioner" caused opponents to take notice.

At every stage, Hopkins stayed focused. He refined his training methods. A dedicated "training machine," to this day Hopkins trains 365 days a year. He leads a disciplined life, rising at 5 or 6 a.m. for roadwork, and going to bed at 9 p.m. His gym workouts are intense and legendary, consisting of heavy bag, speed bag, multiple rounds of jump rope, heavy neck weight harness, calisthenics, and work with a medicine ball, in addition to sparring. He doesn't smoke, and has not had a drink since he was 17. His diet is rigid and Spartan, consisting largely of fruits and vegetables, fish, and protein supplements, all of which has combined to produce his 30-inch waist. He is a model of clean living, which he attributes as one important reason for his success in boxing and in life. In addition, he is known to study the sport, techniques, and watches fight films constantly in a continuous effort to improve his craft, and understand the strengths and weaknesses of his opponents, long before they square off in the ring.

Hopkins' hard work paid off at perhaps the most well known moment of his career, when three years after the Trinidad fight, he was victorious over then-champ Oscar De La Hoya. On September 18, 2004, Hopkins knocked out De La Hoya in the ninth round, elevating his status even further and adding the WBO World Middleweight Title to his list of accomplishments.

This turned out to be a fateful meeting for Hopkins, as a

few months after their fight, he and Oscar De La Hoya were to become business partners in Golden Boy Promotions, Oscar's very successful boxing promotion company. Hopkins was appointed head of Golden Boy Promotions East, a branch of Golden Boy Promotions that specializes in the recruitment, development and promotion of East Coast fighters, while also promoting events in the eastern part of the United States.

But the years seemed to be catching up to Hopkins. Now at the age of 40, he was also to again taste defeat. He lost two close fights to Jermaine Taylor in 2005, and his Middleweight Title belts along with them. But then came an important moment of victory; his hard work helped him build the muscle and the weight necessary to step up in weight-class, and win the IBO/NBA Light Heavyweight Titles, and *The Ring* magazine Light Heavyweight Title, in a unanimous decision over Antonio Tarver on June 10, 2006. This victory could have been a great way to retire his gloves, as Hopkins was now 41. And then there was the promise to his mother: before she died, he had promised to retire in his 41st year.

But a funny thing happened to Hopkins on the way to his rocking chair. Restless in retirement and a fighter through and through, he broke that promise to his mother. At the age of 42, he couldn't pass up a chance to take on former champion Winky Wright on July 21, 2007, and won a unanimous decision defending his *The Ring* magazine Light Heavyweight Title over the 35-year-old Wright. Working Bernard's corner that night for the first time was trainer Freddie Roach. Roach observed, "He's a very disciplined person. He lives a disciplined life. He doesn't eat junk food. He doesn't let his weight fluctuate and he takes care of his body. He's never been in any real hard, hard fights where he's taken any beatings. So, 42 may be a high number, but your age in boxing comes from how many wars you've been in . . . Bernard, he's a defensive guy. He doesn't get hit with shots. He's a very fresh 42 and he takes care of himself."[2]

Bernard is probably "fresh" for a reason—his intelligence in the ring, which is another key ingredient to his success. Truly a smart ring tactician, Hopkins fights with the philosophy of taking as little punishment as possible while dishing out as much as he can. There is a great deal of ring artistry and discipline involved in his fights, and he has adapted a style for himself where he receives very little damage, rarely getting hurt.

He then subsequently lost a tough split decision to undefeated Joe Calzaghe on April 19, 2008. Ironically, on occasion Calzaghe uses the name "Terminator" as his ring handle. So it was the "Terminator," Calzaghe, against Hopkins, the "Executioner." Boxing fans loved the match-up, and the fight did not disappoint.

On October 18, 2008, came another career defining fight against Kelly Pavlik, the WBC and WBO World Middleweight Champion, who moved up in weight for this non-title fight with Hopkins, a light heavyweight. Though they were not in same weight classes, and therefore could not fight for Pavlik's Middleweight Titles, each was equally challenged by the reputation and stature of the other. For Pavlik, this was a challenge to fight one of boxing's best without risking his Middleweight

Titles. For Hopkins, it was another chance to prove himself against a younger, highly regarded, undefeated fighter. It was a headline grabbing fight.

Going into this fight, Pavlik was 33-0, with 30 knockouts. Pavlik had previously beaten Jermaine Taylor for his titles, the man who had dethroned Hopkins from his Middleweight Titles. The "smart money" was betting against Hopkins, and the press had Pavlik a heavy favorite. The fight was no contest, as Hopkins "took Pavlik to school" and decisively dominated him from the opening bell. At the end of the fight when the results were read, Hopkins stood facing the press area outside the ring with a cold stare, a silent message of his defiance over their disbelief in his ability to win, which they had voiced in their pre-fight coverage leading up to the event. It was a triumphant moment for Hopkins, who was 43 (which is like 80 in boxing years), winning out over Pavlik, who was 26. By any objective measure, Bernard Hopkins appears to have found a fistic fountain of youth, although it is one of his creation due to the amazing rigor and discipline by which he lives.

Like a well oiled and superbly conditioned machine, Bernard Hopkins journeys on, despite skeptics who question him at every turn, and constantly ask about a future retirement. However, due to the incredibly determined regimen by which he lives, he is in better shape and more prepared for his fight future than men half his age. What does the future hold for Bernard Hopkins? Every day, this master craftsman of the sport still rises no later than 6 a.m., enjoys his bird-like dietary habits, refrains from alcohol, and works out as if he is fighting for a championship the following week. In his non-training moments, he studies fight films. Whatever he decides to do next, the betting line is that he will be very successful. With the power of his focus, he can turn his disciplined ways towards any endeavor he chooses and, with the intense preparation for which he is famous, rise up and meet any challenges he might encounter.

Today, Bernard Hopkins fights on. Well into his 40's, he is as successful and well respected as ever. He is a living example of the power of discipline and preparation to help any man rise above his circumstances, no matter how dire they might be, and achieve success.

Although a boxer's level of commitment is, of necessity, extreme, the quality of preparation is as important in business and all of life's challenges, as it is in the ring. Preparing well for any endeavor in a disciplined and focused manner can give someone the advantage needed in any competitive or opportunistic situation.

JOE LOUIS

Born: May 13, 1914, Lafayette, Alabama
Died: April 12, 1981, Las Vegas, Nevada
Won World Heavyweight Title: June 22, 1937 (defeated James J. Braddock)
Retired as Champion: March 1, 1949
Returned to Ring: September 27, 1950 (never regained title)
Record: 68 wins, 3 losses, 54 knockouts
Boxing Handle: Brown Bomber

MAX SCHMELING

Born: September 28, 1905, Klein-Luckow/Uckermark, Germany
Died: February 2, 2005, Hamburg, Germany
Won Vacant World Heavyweight Title by Disqualification: June 12, 1930 (defeated Jack Sharkey)
Lost World Heavyweight Title: June 21, 1932 (Jack Sharkey)
Record: 56 wins, 10 losses, 4 draws, 40 knockouts
Boxing Handle: Black Uhlan of the Rhine

ROUND ELEVEN

Maintaining Dignity Through Winning and Losing

✦ Joe Louis and Max Schmeling ✦

> . . . you learn more from one loss than you do from a million wins. I mean, it's really tough to shake the hand of someone who just beat you, and even harder to do it with a smile. If you can learn to do this and push through that pain, you will remember what that moment is like the next time you win and have a better sense of how those competitors around you feel.
>
> —Amy Van Dyken, Olympic Gold Medalist, Swimming

Max Schmeling won a great fight against Joe Louis, and then lost one to him in return. Louis, on the other hand, lost a hard fight against Schmeling, and came back to win the next one with a sensational knockout.

What a boxer will do to win, and how he or she handles winning or losing can reveal a great deal about them—their character, their empathy, and their graciousness. The bonding experience between these two boxers, Louis and Schmeling—once determined combatants in the ring—became a supportive, personal, and rewarding friendship when they stepped out of the ring and moved forward with their lives.

Both Louis and Schmeling handled their victories and defeats with dignity and grace. How they treated each other at the conclusion of their epic battles, and then later as they went through life, showed the strength of their inner makeup and character.

✦ ✦ ✦

IN 1936 AND 1938, two great boxers, Joe Louis and Max Schmeling, fought two tough, career defining battles at Yankee Stadium in New York and traded victories. History has chronicled these fights as symbolic of a larger conflict between two opposing nations on the eve of World War II. Fighting during the time of the buildup of the German war machine towards this world conflict, the eyes of the world watched as the man who stood for American freedom and democracy, Louis, squared off against Schmeling, unfairly perceived to be representative of German oppression. While the fights themselves garnered worldwide attention, the true power of their legacy lies in how these opponents handled the aftermath of these contests. In displaying a dignity and mutual respect for each other—before and after their fights—and then throughout the rest of their lives—they set an elevated standard of conduct towards each other that captured the world's attention and admiration.

The paths that these two heroes had taken to arrive at Yankee Stadium for their two legendary struggles had been quite different.

JOE LOUIS

Joseph Louis Barrow, better known as Joe Louis, was born in Lafayette, Alabama, the seventh of eight children of Munroe Barrow, a sharecropper, and Lily Reece Barrow. Joe's parents both took the name of their owner, James Barrow, on whose plantation they lived and worked. Louis had no recollection of his father, who had been sent away to the epileptic ward of Searcy State Hospital for the Negro Insane, where it was later falsely reported that he died (Munroe actually lived on for another twenty years, unaware of his son's boxing successes until near the end of Munroe's life). Believing herself to be a widow, Louis's mother re-married another widower, Pat Brooks, who also had eight children of his own. They were able to scrape together a minimal existence farming cotton, and the Barrow/Brooks children took part whenever they could. Stuttering and stammering as a child, young Joe did not like school, and instead would often opt to help out at home.

The combined families relocated to Detroit in 1926, where Joe's stepfather was able to get a job as a street cleaner. In school, 12-year-old Joe was again struggling academically. Eventually, he was transferred to an all-boys vocational school, where he performed better with tasks such as building furniture, as opposed to studying mathematics or history. In addition, he was able to take home his handmade furniture for his family to use.

There were several gangs in Joe's neighborhood and, as Joe

came to be known for being good with his fists, he was often encouraged by various gang members to join up. Concerned about the company he was occasionally keeping, Joe's mother gave him 50 cents each week for violin lessons, but instead he used the money to join a recreation center where he took up boxing, and soon fell in love with the sport. He was able to borrow enough money from his sister, Emmarell, to obtain boxing equipment, and made her promise not to tell his mother. He left school at age 17 to concentrate on training to box. For money, he hauled coal and sold vegetables, among other odd jobs.

As Joe became a more skilled and more confident boxer, the time came for him to try his luck in an amateur bout. He decided to fight as "Joe Louis," in order to hide his boxing from his family; the name stuck. In his first bout in 1932 at the age of 18, Joe got off to a rough start when he was knocked down seven times in two rounds and decisively lost to former Olympian Johnny Milner. Louis was so deflated that when his stepfather suggested he give up boxing and take a real job, he took his advice. But Louis made it only 2 months at a Ford auto-body plant before he missed boxing so much that he had to return to the sport. Joe recommitted himself to the amateur circuit and met with great success.

He captured the attention of a highly regarded, local manager named John Roxborough, who, after providing Louis with clothes, boxing equipment and pocket money, introduced him to manager Julian Black, who would co-manage Louis with Roxborough. Black was a gambler and had a stable of black fighters in Chicago, where he sent Joe to begin training with Jack "Chappie" Blackburn. Blackburn placed Louis on a strict training regimen designed to build a clean-living image for Louis that would make him accepted in white society, and in sharp contrast to Jack Johnson, the first American black champion, who held the World Heavyweight Title from 1908–1915, but had flaunted himself among society by consorting with prostitutes and marrying white women. Blackburn also told Louis that he would have to be twice as good as a white boxer to get anywhere in the sport—a challenge that Louis readily accepted. As an amateur, Joe compiled an amateur record of 50-4, with 43 knockouts, winning the Light Heavyweight Title in the National AAU and the Detroit Golden Gloves.

His first professional boxing match occurred on July 4, 1934 with a first round knockout of Jack Kracken. He had 12 professional fights in 1934, winning them all, ten by knockout. Joe was getting a great deal of attention from the press, and he was given a number of nicknames—among them: "Alabama Assassin," "Detroit Destroyer," "the Michigan Mauler," "Brown Bomber," "the Dark Destroyer," and the "Coffee-Colored Kayo King." The "Brown Bomber" stuck for the rest of his career.

In 1935, Mike Jacobs picked up his contract as sole promoter for the next three years, and Joe's life began to change dramatically, as Jacobs, the owner of the Twentieth Century Club, a Madison Square Garden rival, was able to give him the exposure he needed. Louis won his first 27 fights, 23 by knockout, defeating the likes of former Heavyweight Champions Primo Carnera and Max Baer. Louis had very quickly established himself as a serious contender for the title. In less than three years, Joe had come a very long way from his 25 dollars per week job at the Ford plant. As his fight with Schmeling was approaching, Louis was a newfound celebrity in the ring and was susceptible to becoming overly confident. Boldly, Louis promised that he would make a quick victory over Schmeling. He couldn't have known what was in store for him, or predicted how this fight would change his life.

MAX SCHMELING

Maximillian Adolph Otto Siegfried Schmeling grew up in Hamburg, Germany, where he honed his athletic abilities by participating in track, wrestling and soccer. Young Max became interested in boxing in his early teenage years after seeing a film of the Heavyweight Championship fight between Jack Dempsey and Georges Carpentier. After buying a pair of secondhand gloves, Max taught himself how to box. He turned professional in 1924, at age 19, and started winning fights that same year.

From 1926 through 1928, he won the German Light Heavyweight Title, the European Light Heavyweight Title, and the German Heavyweight Title. He came to New York in 1929, and defeated a pair of top heavyweights, Johnny Risko and Paolino Uzcudun, making him the number two contender for the World Heavyweight Title at the time. Known as a thoughtful, cleaver ring tactician with a solid punch, he built a record 42 wins with 30 knockouts, 4 losses and 3 draws before defeating Jack Sharkey (by disqualification) at Yankee Stadium on June 12, 1930, for the World Heavyweight Title.

Despite his good looks, Max Schmeling was a shy man amidst the glitter and tumultuous times of Berlin's "Golden Twenties." In 1932, he married a blond, beautiful movie star, Anny Ondra (Anna Sophie Ondrakova), and the two became Germany's most glamorous couple in a marriage that lasted 54 years until her death in 1987.

Schmeling was a decent man who became intertwined in conflict with the Nazi regime and radical policies of Hitler's Third Reich. Hitler was a big proponent of boxing, having extolled it in *Mein Kampf*, and insisting it be taught in German schools. Though Schmeling wasn't a Nazi, he was often unfairly linked to Nazism, and his visit to the U.S. for these contests was encouraged and closely followed by Adolf Hitler, who saw Schmeling as a symbol of a superior Aryan race. On several occasions, Hitler made personal overtures to enlist Schmeling to join the Nazi Party, but Schmeling refused. Despite the repeated insistence of Joseph Goebbels, master propagandist of the Nazi regime, Schmeling also refused to stop associating with German Jews or fire his American Jewish manager, Joe Jacobs.

By the time Schmeling met Louis in the ring in 1936, he had won (in 1930) and lost (in 1932) the World Heavyweight Championship to Jack Sharkey. Schmeling then lost a tough battle in 1933 by TKO to Max Baer, who was to win the World Heavyweight Championship one year later. Then leading up to the first bout with Louis, Schmeling fought mostly in Europe.

THE LEGENDARY FIGHTS

With renowned knockout power in both hands, Joe Louis had become accustomed to winning, and was a 10-1 favorite in the first fight with Max Schmeling in 1936. Days before the fight he was found playing golf, rather than in the gym training hard. Schmeling, on the other hand, had studied Louis' style intently and proclaimed that he had found a chink in Louis' armor, observing (to himself) the way Louis dropped his left hand after he doubled up on the jab. Schmeling told the press in advance of the fight "I see something."

Louis and Schmeling met for their first match at Yankee Stadium in the Bronx, New York, on June 19, 1936. With approximately 40,000 people in attendance, the gate was only half what was expected for their first bout, due to a variety of *factors*, including boycott by a Jewish organization, high ticket prices, and rain which postponed the fight. In the fourth round, Schmeling proved that he had in fact seen "something" vulnerable in Louis: he honed in on the Brown Bomber and dropped him with his overhand right once Louis had momentarily dropped his guard after a punch. This was the first time Louis had been floored in his professional career. From that moment on, it was nearly impossible for Louis to completely regain his ring composure. During the rest of the bout, he fought unsteadily, and was knocked out by Schmeling in the 12th round. The world was shocked, and the effects of the outcome rippled across America and the Atlantic.

The loss delivered a hard blow to Louis' American fans, particularly the black community—there was rioting in Harlem following the bout. The Nazis shamelessly used the outcome of this first fight to turn the event into a propaganda pitch for Aryan supremacy during the 1936 Olympic Games in Berlin. As for Louis himself, the sting of defeat and the guilt of disappointing his followers was acute; he cried in his dressing room after the loss. Meanwhile, Schmeling was flown back to Germany on the brand-new, futuristic airship *Hindenberg*, where he was honored by his fellow Germans. Hitler sent Schmeling a telegram congratulating him on his victory, and later hosted him for a weekend at Berchtesgarden, his mountain retreat in the Bavarian Alps. As the reality of what had happened set in, the world might never have imagined that they could ever become friends—one man was utterly defeated, and the other a triumphant champion.

Following his humiliating loss in the first bout with Schmeling, Louis returned to his training with a renewed purpose—to defeat Max Schmeling in a rematch. Along the way, he gained the title of Heavyweight Champion of the World after knocking out Jimmy Braddock on June 22, 1937. Despite this victory, Louis said he could not consider himself to be a true champion until he had avenged his loss to Schmeling.

When Louis and Schmeling met in the ring for the second time on June 22, 1938, the Second World War was looming on the horizon, and the whole world was watching. Yankee Stadium was sold out with over 70,000 in attendance, and millions tuned into the match, which was broadcast by radio all over the United States and Germany. The threat of war was real, and the fighters' confrontation came to symbolize the impending conflict between Germany and the United States. Despite his public opposition to Nazism, Schmeling became associated with everything that Americans despised about the menacing political regime of Germany, and needed even more protection from the contentious crowd than when he had met Louis two years prior. As he made his way to the ring, 25 police officers were assigned to protect Schmeling from the hostile crowd that mercilessly pummeled him with everything from cigarette butts and paper cups, to ashtrays and banana peels.

The fight was quick and powerful as Louis scored a dramatic first round knockout. Touching perfection in the ring that night, Louis knocked Schmeling down three times in the 124-second bout that transcended the sport. As anxious fans listened to this news in Germany, the radio broadcast there was mysteriously cut off and replaced by music when it became obvious that Schmeling was in serious trouble and would likely lose the fight.

Louis' 1938 defeat of Schmeling was a defining moment in black history, as it confirmed that there indeed is no such thing as white supremacy, despite the convictions and propaganda of Adolf Hitler and the Nazi regime. But of even more significance was that Louis came to be respected as a national hero and sports icon, not only in the African-American community, but to all Americans. In their fervent support of Louis'victory over Schmeling, the entire country had united despite race, gender, and class to support Louis' symbolic defeat of Nazi Germany as unfairly embodied by Max Schmeling. It was a shining moment for Louis and the nation. Years later, boxing historian Randy Roberts simply stated, "This was the biggest fight in the history of the world."[1]

As a result of one of Louis' punches, thrown when Schmeling had turned to his side to avoid Louis' attack, Schmeling had split a vertebrae in two places and was sent to a nearby hospital to recover, where he would remain for 10 days. As a gesture of concern and sportsmanship, Schmeling attempted to visit Louis during his hospital stay but was refused. Schmeling later said in his autobiography, ". . . I wasn't allowed to have visitors—no reporters, no friends, not even Joe Louis. When he tried to visit me, (managers) Joe Jacobs and Max Machon wouldn't allow it . . . I was too out of it to get involved."[2]

Despite the physical damage he had endured, a mutual respect developed between Louis and Schmeling—a dynamic that they would eventually carry with them for the remainder of their lives. After his recovery, Schmeling returned to Germany as a disgraced man, having lost face with Hitler and among his fellow Germans after the embarrassing loss to a black man. Their lives were to take dramatically different paths after these fights, as the world rushed to war. But the relationship which they had embarked upon would endure.

THE AFTERMATH

After his loss to Louis in 1938, Hitler turned against Schmeling and, as punishment for his refusal to join the Nazi Party, had

Schmeling drafted into the German Air Force (Luftwaffe), as an elite paratrooper (Fallschirmjager). Schmeling managed to survive the war, but didn't recover from his encounter with Louis as easily, as he had recurring injuries to his back as a result of the damage inflicted by Louis in their second fight. At the end of the war, the British authorities cleared Schmeling of any complicity with Nazi crimes.

When the United States entered World War II following the Japanese attack on Pearl Harbor, Joe enlisted in the U.S. Army on January 10, 1942 and served as a Private from 1942 to 1945, while also fighting in almost 100 exhibition matches. During the war years, he was able to utilize his hero status and became a symbol of democracy as he toured from base to base in the U.S. Army, speaking to troops to build morale and raise money for the military forces. Despite being ordered to perform before segregated audiences, he refused to do so and was widely quoted in appearances before the military to have said, "We're going to win because we are on God's side," which struck a note of true patriotism to many an American, both in and out of uniform. By the end of the war, Joe Louis had been promoted to Sergeant, and had traveled over 70,000 miles and visited almost five million servicemen.

In Louis' attempts to help the war effort, he had donated his entire winnings from two title fights to the Army and Navy Relief Funds, without deducting taxes beforehand. At the end of the war, Louis consequently found that he was in debt to the IRS for approximately $100,000 in unpaid taxes—a debt that was interest bearing, and continued to grow. After the war ended, Louis had another 14 fights, after which he retired as Heavyweight Champion on March 1, 1949, but was forced to reenter the ring in 1950, in order to earn money to pay the IRS. By 1951, with interest and penalties, his debt to the IRS stood near $1 million. To help pay off his debt, Louis signed to fight for the Heavyweight Championship against Rocky Marciano on October 26, 1951, for a guaranteed $300,000. He was defeated soundly by Marciano, and finally retired from the boxing ring for good. Despite his best efforts, Louis remained under pressure on the debt burden he shouldered until the 1960's when the government under President John F. Kennedy gave him relief on the payments on past obligations, although the debt was never officially forgiven.

Louis and Schmeling were to meet again in 1954 when Schmeling returned to the U.S. to referee a bout in Milwaukee, Wisconsin. On this trip, Schmeling traveled to Chicago to find Louis, where the two men reminisced, even appearing together on the popular television program, "This is Your Life."

The final chapters for Joe Louis were difficult for him. He would do anything to raise money to satisfy his obligations to the IRS, and even had a stint as a professional wrestler. In many ways, he appeared to have outlived his time and seemed out of place. He had trouble adjusting to the black athletes of the 60's and 70's who were more vocal and impatient than he, such as Muhammad Ali. He did not share their rage, and they did not share his humility.

Things began to darken further for Louis towards the late 60's. He became depressed, hospitalized, and there were also reports of his drug use and bouts with paranoia. He was released and became a greeter for $50,000 per year at Caesar's Palace in Las Vegas, a position he enjoyed, as he was back in the public eye, and everyone wanted to meet him and shake his hand. He developed heart problems in 1977, later had a stroke, and was confined to a wheelchair in his final years. He was quietly aided financially by Schmeling, who helped pay his medical bills. They ended up seeing each other about a dozen times from that 1954 reunion until Louis died on April 11, 1981, one month from his 67th birthday.

Louis did not qualify for burial in Arlington Cemetery, but President Reagan waived the requirements, and he was buried with full military honors. Recognized as a champion for freedom, his burial in Arlington signified the enormous contributions he had made to his country. Present at his funeral, for which he helped pay, was Schmeling, who served as a pallbearer.

One of the ironies in their stories is what happened to Schmeling and Louis financially throughout their lives. After the war, they were both broke. Schmeling's post-war boxing successes and farming concerns allowed him to regain a financial toehold in a Germany that was in ruins following the war. Schmeling used his prize winnings from the revival of his boxing career to purchase the German distributorship of Atlanta-based Coca Cola Company, which allowed him to make millions. He became a successful businessman, grew wealthy in the postwar era, and became one of Germany's most respected philanthropists. In an ironic twist of fate, Joe Louis, who had been the symbol of democracy and a spokesman for the Allied war effort, ended up with nothing, and was hounded by the U.S. government for payment of back taxes. Both carried their respective fates with pride and humility, neither boasting nor complaining whichever way life took them.

The humblest of men, the grandson of slaves, Louis was a soft-spoken champion who left a mark of huge social significance and set the standard for what was to follow in the succeeding decades of athletic competition. He loved his country despite all, and by his example, he helped move America forward—in doing so, he was able to lift the standards and aspirations of all.

Schmeling was known to treasure friendships, and each of his ring opponents became his friends over the course of his life—whether he won or lost to them. He was named German Athlete of the Century, and his star-power seemed to continually advance as he got older. He set up a charitable foundation to raise money for the poor and elderly.

"'That's my hobby—making money on the one hand and giving it away with the other,' he once said."[3] When he passed away on February 2, 2005, seven months shy of his hundredth birthday, he was revered not only as one of Germany's most respected sports figures who had achieved incredible athletic accomplishments, but also for his humility, character, generosity, and humanitarianism.

Schmeling stuck by Louis like a brother, no matter how impoverished, enfeebled or displaced Louis became. He crossed the ocean repeatedly to appear by his side, and showered him with praises born of respect and true admiration. Louis, in turn, embraced his friendship, and welcomed his attention. Perhaps the saga of Joe Louis and Max Schmeling, and the respect and loyalty they had for each other, born in the throes of athletic competition, can be summarized in what Max was to say when Joe had passed on, "I didn't like him . . . I loved him."[4]

Life is full of battles, big and small. No one wins them all. This is also true of boxing, as even great boxers will typically lose several times during their career. It is no secret that losing is a part of life—whether in boxing, politics, business or any other human endeavor. Of course, we all live to win—everyone admires the champion tennis player, the fastest runner, the winning college debater, or successful politician. Winners are respected, revered. Losing at anything can feel embarrassing, frustrating and difficult to swallow. Some people get mad at losing, while others, unable to cope, retreat from view for sustained periods.

Joe Louis and Max Schmeling demonstrated that there are those who can handle a loss with grace and poise, living to fight another day—eventually leading the way to other victories, and showing to all the path of true sportsmanship and mutual respect. Today, it is the world's knowledge of the content of their character, as well as their performance in the ring, that make their fights classics in the history of the sport. There is much to be learned from Louis and Schmeling, and how they handled their respective victories and defeats with humility and pride, both as young boxing champions and later throughout their lives as they grew to be older, wiser men.

The greatest accomplishment is not in never falling, but in rising again after you fall.

—Vince Lombardi, Hall of Fame football coach

VITALI KLITSCHKO

Born: July 19, 1971, Belovodsk, Kyrgyzstan, Soviet Union

Won WBO Heavyweight Title: June 26, 1999 (defeated Herbie Hide)

Lost WBO Heavyweight Title: April 1, 2000 (Chris Byrd)

Won WBC Heavyweight Title: April 24, 2004 (defeated Corrie Sanders)

Retired: November 9, 2005, due to a knee injury

Won WBC Heavyweight Title: October 11, 2008 (defeated Samuel Peter)

Record: 37 wins, 2 losses, 36 knockouts

Boxing Handle: Dr. Ironfist

WLADIMIR KLITSCHKO

Born: March 25, 1976, Semipalatinsk, Kazakhstan, Soviet Union

WBO Heavyweight Title: October 14, 2000 (defeated Chris Byrd)

Lost WBO Heavyweight Title: March 8, 2003 (Corrie Sanders)

Won IBF & vacant IBO Heavyweight Titles: April 22, 2006 (defeated Chris Byrd)

Won WBO Heavyweight Title: February 23, 2008 (defeated Sultan Ibragimov)

Record: 53 wins, 3 losses, 47 knockouts

Boxing Handle: Dr. Steelhammer

ROUND TWELVE—THE CHAMPIONSHIP ROUND

Giving Back

✦ Vitali and Wladimir Klitschko ✦

I've always respected those who tried to change the world for the better, rather than just complain about it.

—Michael Bloomberg, Founder of Bloomberg L.P., and Mayor of New York City

In the ring, the Klitschko brothers are impressive and accomplished. Combined, they currently hold four of the five World Heavyweight Championship belts, dominating boxing's heavyweight division, historically regarded as the most prestigious prize in sports. But through the sport of boxing, they have accomplished even more, using their achievements as a platform to provide generous support to organizations which carry forth their philanthropic interests, as well as to advance ambitions for public service. In these efforts, they have given unselfishly of their time, as well as their money.

Wladimir and Vitali Klitschko know that success isn't just about winning; it's also about finding ways to help others less fortunate, and at the same time, using their resources and talents to improve the world in which we live.

✦ ✦ ✦

SONS OF A Soviet Air Force Colonel, Vitali and Wladimir Klitschko were raised in a middle class background. Because their father, Vladimir Rodionovich, was reassigned to different military posts, the brothers were born in different locations: Vitali in Belovodsk, Kyrgyz SSR, Soviet Union (now Kyrgyzstan), and Wladimir in Semipalatinsk, Kazakhstan. The family settled in Kiev, Ukraine. Five years apart in age (Vitali is the older), the brothers' upbringing was the antithesis of the rough and tumble background of many boxers: their mother was a teacher and emphasized the importance of learning, and both boys began playing chess at an early age. Even as young men, Vitali and Wladimir have a litany of successes and accomplishments, both in and out of the ring.

The brothers got their start in boxing as teenagers. Although he always admired former World Heavyweight Champion Max Schmeling, Vitali never dreamed as a boy that he would become a professional boxer. Nevertheless, at age 13, Vitali began his martial arts career as a kick boxer, and was a six-time world champion, twice as an amateur and four times as a professional. Eventually, he also added boxing to his repertoire, and, as an amateur, was Ukrainian Heavyweight Champion three times. In 1995, at age 24, as a boxer he won the silver medal as a super heavyweight at the amateur world championships and also won the Super Heavyweight gold medal at the first World Military Games that same year (his brother Wladimir won the Heavyweight Title at the same contest.) Vitali concluded his amateur boxing career with a record of 195-15, with 80 knockouts.

With his older brother's accomplishments as a boxer serving as a role model, Wladimir became interested in boxing at the age of 14. In 1993 at age 17, Wladimir became the champion of Europe among juniors. One year later, he received the silver medal at the Junior World Championships in Istanbul, Turkey. In 1995, at age 19, he won the heavyweight gold medal at the Military World Championships in Ariccia, Italy. In 1996, at age 20, he captured second place as a Super Heavyweight at the European Championships. Along the way, Wladimir was also a five time Heavyweight Champion of the Ukraine. These were quite the accomplishments, especially for someone who, as a youth, dreamed of being a doctor and never fantasized about being a boxer.

Also in 1996, the Olympic authorities in the Ukraine looked to Vitali, 25, and Wladimir, 20, to represent their country at the upcoming Olympic Games in Atlanta. Vitali was to box as a super heavyweight; Wladimir as heavyweight. Unfortunately, Vitali was disqualified on a technicality. However, this opened the door for Wladimir to fight as a super heavyweight (a welcome opportunity, as Wladimir had been struggling to make weight in the heavyweight category.) As a super heavyweight, Wladimir faced four tough opponents, the first of whom was Lawrence Clay-Bey of the United States. Wladimir won a close decision at 10-8.

Wladimir's final Olympic and amateur match was against Paea Wolfgramm, a former rugby player from Tonga, a country with only 106,000 people spread over 169 islands. After two rounds, Wladimir was only ahead 3-2, but in the third and final round the Ukrainian took four points to Wolfgramm's one, ending the fight with a 7-3 win. Wladimir was now an Olympic gold medalist at age 20. With his victory over Wolfgramm, Wladimir concluded an outstanding amateur career with a 134-6 record, with 65 knockouts.

As impressive as were their accomplishments in the ring, the brothers did not lose their focus on the importance of education. In 1996, the same year he won the Olympic gold medal, Wladimir joined Vitali in being accepted to the post-graduate study program of Kiev University, where both were awarded Ph.D.'s in Sports Science. Influenced by his own preparation for the Olympics as a young man, Wladimir's doctoral thesis focused on scientific study of the preparation of 14-to-17-year-olds who engage in amateur sports. In addition to holding advanced degrees, the brothers also became fluent in four languages, Ukraine, Russian, German and English. In a way, the brothers' interest in education hearkens back to the era of academic excellence of former World Heavyweight Champion Gene Tunney.

Following the Olympics, both brothers moved to Hamburg, Germany in 1996, where they turned pro. Vitali moved through the heavyweight division with an impressive string of knockouts, capturing the WBO Heavyweight Title with a second round KO of Herbie Hide on June 26, 1999. One year later, he lost the title due to a shoulder injury in a fight with Chris Byrd, despite the fact that he was well ahead on all three judges' scorecards when the bout was halted. On June 21, 2003, Vitali gave then-champion Lennox Lewis the scare of his life in a battle for the WBC and IBF Heavyweight Titles. Unfortunately, just when Vitali was gaining momentum in the ring, leading on all three scorecards, the referee stopped the fight due to a severe cut under Vitali's left eyebrow which, the ref ascertained, might have caused permanent damage. Once again, Vitali was ahead on the judges' scorecards when the bout was stopped. However, this near-miss in defeating Lennox Lewis indelibly carved Vitali's credibility in the heavyweight boxing rankings of the era.

After the fight with Lennox Lewis, Vitali continued his ascension in the sport. With every fight, he just kept knocking everyone out: he scored TKO victories over Kirk Johnson on December 6, 2003; and again in April 2004 against Corrie Sanders—a fight in which he won the WBC Heavyweight Title vacated after Lennox Lewis retired on February 6, 2004 (a retirement which, some speculate, might have been hastened by the tough battle which Lennox had with Vitali). After scoring a TKO victory over Danny Williams on December 11, 2004, Vitali underwent knee surgery, and then retired on November 9, 2005.

But, after recovering from surgery and consulting with his doctors, Vitali returned to the ring in 2007. This was part of a dream that he and his brother Wladimir had shared for many years—to write their own passage in boxing history by having two brothers hold world championship titles at the same time. Vitali's return was sweet and the brothers' dream was realized on October 11, 2008, when Vitali beat defending champion Samuel Peter, and reclaimed the WBC title he had surrendered upon his retirement. Vitali holds the distinction of being one of the few Heavyweight Champions never to have been knocked down professionally. He has an extremely high knockout percentage, having scored 36 knockout victories (out of 37 wins) in 39 professional fights (92%). One cannot help but compare his record to Rocky Marciano, another Heavyweight Champion with a high knockout percentage, whose final knockout rate stood at 88% with 43 knockouts in 49 fights.

Like his older brother, Wladimir wasted no time entering the professional ranks. After reaching professional status, Wladimir easily won his first 24 fights, mostly by knockout, before he suffered his first loss to Ross Puritty in Hamburg, Germany on December 5, 1998. He then won his next 16 fights, picking up the WBO Championship belt on October 14, 2000, in a unanimous decision over Chris Byrd, who he knocked down twice in the contest. At that time, Wladimir was being considered as a legitimate opponent for Lennox Lewis, who held the other Heavyweight Title belts, but after losing to Corrie Sanders in 2003 in a disappointing second-round knockout, Wladimir was out of the running. With these losses on his record, Wladimir's ability to take a punch and ring stamina were called into question.

Enter Emanuel Steward, Hall of Fame trainer. Specializing in working with heavyweights, Steward had trained Lennox Lewis, among numerous other world champions. Though Wladimir was to lose one more fight in a fifth round stoppage from Lamon Brewster on April 10, 2004, with Emanuel in his corner, things began to turn around. Emanuel focused on Wladimir's balance and footwork, and worked with him on developing his left jab. Emanuel emphasized more sparring in preparation for bouts, in addition to the conditioning exercises which Wladimir had concentrated on for his training. It worked. The younger Klitschko snapped back with an important victory against Samuel Peter on September 24, 2005, and then captured the IBF and IBO Heavyweight belts with a seventh round TKO over Chris Byrd on April 22, 2006. It has been win, win, win ever since for Wladimir, and he reclaimed the WBO Championship belt with a unanimous decision over Sultan Ibragimov on February 23, 2008, increasing his total world championship belt count to three.

Today, Wladimir and Vitali Klitschko are among the most unique and interesting figures on the world boxing scene. For some time now, they have been viewed as the "new generation" of heavyweights who would follow Lennox Lewis. Currently, the brothers continue to fight out of Hamburg, Germany, where their motivation has not slowed; as Vitali states, "Our ambition is to win every Heavyweight Championship belt and to hold it in the family."[1] With a combined 90 wins in professional boxing, 83 by knockout, they are certainly among the most successful boxers in the game, i.e., one of the best one-two combinations in the business! They have indeed written a unique chapter into boxing history: never before have two brothers dominated a single division the way they have—the Klitschko brothers now hold four of the five World

Heavyweight Title belts (WBC, WBO, IBF, and IBO). Only the WBA remains out of their grasp, currently held by the Russian boxer Nikolay Valuev. But, as the Klitschko brothers continue their meteoric ascent in the boxing arena, it is also clear that, to them, real success, and true accomplishment, means giving back.

In addition to the confidence and humility that the two brothers consistently display, one cannot help but be impressed by their commitment and attitude towards philanthropy. Among other measures, Wladimir has said that he wants to use the sport of boxing in the way that Muhammad Ali did—to use his physical attributes and boxing skills to open doors and make contributions to the world and to society. Wladimir donated $285,000 from his purse for the Calvin Brock fight in November of 2006 to causes directed towards alleviating the menace of AIDS in Namibia; the brothers were taken by the plight of the youth there. This is not the first time this type of charitable generosity has occurred in heavyweight history: the practice of donating fight purses to charity was championed by the great Joe Louis in his day.

In particular, the brothers believe in the power and promise of a good education and, for them, some of their greatest accomplishments center around work with charities dedicated to supporting the needs of schools, churches, and children. Their contributions know no borders, and they make efforts to improve the lives of children around the world. It is estimated that Wladimir was responsible, either from his own purse or from funds raised from fans, for donations of approximately $500,000 from his Heavyweight Championship fight with Sultan Ibragimov in February 2008 to an organization named The Laureus Sport for Good Foundation. Through the support of nearly 50 iconic athletes (including Edwin Moses and John McEnroe, to Boris Becker and Nadia Comaneci), this global charity funds and promotes the use of sport as a tool for social change. In doing so, Laureus also highlights the plight of underprivileged children. It currently supports 51 other programs around the world.

Wladimir has also encouraged others to give back. For example, in his championship fight with Ibragamov, Wladimir encouraged his fans to get involved with Laureus by inviting them to "step in to the ring" with him that night at Madison Square Garden. When fans donated to Laureus, their names were embroidered on the scarlet-colored robe which he wore as he entered the ring. Fans jumped at the chance to give, and to be a part of Wladimir's important title defense: more than 2,000 people donated and were "in Wladimir's corner." Furthermore, the robe was later auctioned off to benefit The Laureus Sport for Good Foundation.

Part of his gift to the The Laureus Sport for Good Foundation went to support an academy by the name of the Betances Boxing Program in the Bronx, New York, which teaches children aged eight and up to box. For over 12 years, the program has served as an alternative for hundreds of kids who face the harsh realities and disadvantages of the low socio-economic strata of those living within the NYC Housing Authority, such as absentee parents, domestic violence, drugs and substance abuse, and the general dangers on the streets of New York City. Betances provides a positive atmosphere and, in addition to teaching the kids how to box, the program acts as a safe haven and provides children life skills, values workshops and academic support.

The brothers do more than give their own money; they get personally involved. In 2002, the Klitschko brothers announced that they had agreed to work for UNESCO (United Nations Educational, Scientific, and Cultural Organization) which supports more than 180 projects in 87 countries. UNESCO pays special attention and commits vast resources to international education. Through this organization, they have been able to help children in Africa, Asia, and South America. In 2002, they supported a project in Brazil. In 2004 and 2005, the brothers lent support to a UNESCO project in Romania. Additionally, in August of 2006, the Klitschko brothers traveled to Namibia to promote educational activities for the children of the San community, who are among the most isolated and underprivileged in the north and west of the country. Alongside these efforts, they have created several foundations in the Ukraine that benefit children and sport.

As an additional way to contribute to society and the world in which he lives, Vitali has embarked on a career in public service, and has channeled his energies towards becoming involved in politics. His intentions are to use politics as a means to provide a positive influence on his hometown of Kiev, where he now lives with his wife and three children. His efforts have focused on the city's political system, which he feels is corrupted and in need of serious reform, and to help make Ukraine a country with European standards of living. In 2006 at the age of 34, he ran for mayor of Kiev. Campaigning on an anti-corruption platform, Vitali placed second in the multi-candidate race, and, during the same election, was elected as a people's deputy to the Kiev City Council. He ran again for the mayoral post in 2008, and was disappointed a second time.

The usually soft-spoken Vitali has been a very vocal critic of the political management of the issues facing the Ukrainian capital and its weakening economy. He has been advised in the political arena by the ex-mayor of New York City, Rudy Giuliani, whose firm, Giuliani Partners, has given Vitali advice on how to turn Kiev around by reforming city government.

The Klitschko brothers continue to provide leadership in world causes. Certainly, much lies ahead for them. They are in an advantageous position to do a great deal of good for the world they live in, at the same time that they continue to rise in the ring (don't count on them fighting each other to unify the heavyweight belts; the brothers made a promise to their mother that they would never fight each other). Boxing is always in need of exemplary citizens to represent the sport, and pugilism is fortunate to be represented by the Klitschko brothers. Together, as friends and brothers, they are dedicated to using their reach to make a difference in the world—for the good.

✦ ✦ ✦

With boxers like Wladimir and Vitali Klitschko in a leadership role, the sport of boxing has ambassadors who understand the necessary responsibility to give something back to the world which has been so good to them.

The same is true for all of us. When great success is achieved by anyone in any profession or endeavor, it is tempting to "take the money and run," and forget about those less fortunate. Yet it is often the most successful people in business, athletics, the arts, and politics who have the chance to be very influential on behalf of much needed charity towards others less fortunate.

The Klitschko Brothers present a better face for boxing at a time when the sport can most definitely use a boost, and set an example for all of us. By their actions, they have demonstrated that they understand a sense of one's place in history and the scheme of things—that opportunities must be shared for others and that, ultimately, one's good fortunes are a matter of chance and circumstance, as well as effort.

Such a perspective on life makes up a sense of humility that breeds true self-knowledge.

A Final Word

THE 12 PRECEDING stories are extraordinary examples from boxing. They highlight how one circumstance—a chance meeting, a fight event, a defeat, a victory—can change a life *forever*. They also make clear that it is only *through a long hard climb that one reaches the top of anything.*

To succeed in the ring – indeed, to succeed in life – once must overcome a unique set of individual challenges. The boxers you have read about were able to convert whatever came their way to success and glory—and, in most cases, in both life *and* in the ring.

All 15 of these boxers had something in them that made them a winner—a toughness, an ability to hang in despite setbacks, a willingness to go for it all.

To say that boxing is *exactly* like life itself is, perhaps, extreme. But life in the ring offers so many comparisons which mirror life itself that I cannot deny the connection.

Rules and Weight Classes

A QUICK SUMMARY OF the rules in boxing is an ambitious undertaking, as today, boxing is governed by state boxing commissions, who also impose physical requirements for participants and professional standards for judges and referees. Professional bouts can be staged up to 12 three-minute rounds (for fights with a championship belt at stake). Fights can be won by knockout (KO), where a fighter is knocked down and cannot get off the canvas, a technical knockout (TKO) where a fighter cannot regain sufficient composure to continue the fight for 10 seconds after being injured or knocked down by his opponent, or a majority decision of three independent judges. There is one minute for the fighters to rest in between rounds. The fight can be ruled a win, a loss, a draw, or a no-decision, depending on the ruling of the judges. A doctor is always present at ringside, and the "third man" in the ring is an independent referee.

There are various rules and ring courtesies which are to be observed. There are stringent guidelines on how boxers are to conduct themselves: there is to be no hitting below the belt (waistline), no gouging in the eyes, no biting, no kicking, no hitting after the bell at the end of the round, no rabbit punching (hitting behind the head), no hitting on the break (after boxers have clinched), and others. Points can be deducted by the referee if violations occur.

Fights are conducted in a squared ring to be no less than 22 feet square, and no greater than 24 feet square. A fighter can have a corner man or trainer to advise him before the fight, and between rounds. He can also have someone present to administer medical attention in the event of cuts or other injuries, who is referred to as a "cutman."

The success of boxers has always been associated with their size, i.e., the bigger the man, the harder he was to "beat" in a boxing match. As a result, there are many weight classes in professional boxing today. For men, there are 17 weight classifications, per the designations of one of the regulatory bodies that oversee the sport, the IBF.

Heavyweight—Above 200 pounds
Cruiserweight—not over 200 pounds
Light Heavyweight—not over 175 pounds
Super Middleweight—not over 168 pounds
Middleweight—not over 160 pounds
Junior Middleweight—not over 154 pounds
Welterweight—not over 147 pounds
Junior Welterweight—not over 140 pounds
Lightweight—not over 135 pounds
Junior Lightweight—not over 130 pounds
Featherweight—not over 126 pounds
Junior Featherweight—not over 122 pounds

Bantamweight—not over 118 pounds
Junior Bantamweight—not over 115
Flyweight—not over 112 pounds
Junior Flyweight—not over 108 pounds
Mini Flyweight—not over 105 pounds

Of course, weight classifications for women have lower thresholds, and are regulated by the IFBA and WIBA.

When professional fights are arranged, they are done by weight class, meaning that the boxer's weight cannot exceed the guidelines above. Therefore, a boxer must "make weight," meaning he must come in either at or below the cutoff for the particular weight class. For example, someone fighting at the middleweight level cannot exceed 160 pounds at the "weigh-in" which occurs a day or two before the actual match.

See the Boxing Glossary on page 177 for more specific terms and definitions mentioned here, and generally associated with the sport.

Boxing Glossary

A

Alphabet Soup

Alphabet soup refers to the abbreviations of the numerous boxing sanctioning bodies such as IBA, IBO, NABA, NABC, NABF, WBF, WBO, etc. that have sprung up since the 1980s that sponsor championship fights and hand out title belts for 17 different weight classes.

B

Barnburner

A barnburner is a very good fight—one that is very intense and exciting, a real nail-biter. A fight that is so close it's hard to predict who will come out the winner until seconds before it ends.

Below the Belt

Below the belt is an imaginary line from the belly button to the top of the hips where a boxer is not supposed to hit. To hit below the belt is to not behave according to the rules or decency.

Body Punches

Body punches, particularly a left hook delivered to the floating rib area (the bottom of the rib cage and towards the side) where the liver, is can stop a fighter if landed perfectly. Body punches delivered not quite so precisely but repeatedly round after round wear a boxer down. A sore gut, bruised ribs make it hard to breathe.

Bout

A bout is a boxing match consisting of rounds with one-minute breaks between rounds.

Boxers Handshake

Touching knuckles is how boxers greet each other whether they're wearing gloves or not. Touching gloves before the opening bell is also part of boxing protocol.

Boxing Commission

Boxing commission is an entity authorized under state law to regulate professional boxing matches.

Brawler

A brawler is a slugger. It's a boxer who lacks finesse in the ring, moves slower, lacks mobility, has a predictable punching pattern, but makes up for all that with raw power and the ability to knockout their opponents with a single punch.

C

Clinch

A clinch is a last resort defensive technique. It's when one boxer holds onto the other to avoid being hit or muffle an opponent's attack.

Combination

A combination is a series of punches thrown in sequence like a left jab, followed by a straight right, followed by a left hook.

Corner Man

At the junction of the ropes where a boxer rests between rounds his second, the corner man, advises him, gives him water, tries to reduce swelling and stop bleeding.

Count

A count is tolling of the seconds by the referee after a boxer is knocked down. If a boxer is still down at the end of the count of 10 then the fight is over by knockout.

Counterpunch

A counterpuncher waits for his opponent to throw a punch, blocks or slips past them, and then exploits the opening in the opponent's position with a counter attack or punch.

Cross

A cross is a power punch thrown with the boxer's dominant hand. It's also called a straight right, right or straight punch.

Cut Man

Someone present in a fighter's corner to administer medical attention in the event of cuts or other injuries.

D

Dirty Fighting

Holding an opponent's head down and hitting face with uppercuts or ribs with hooks, rabbit punches, elbowing, forearm in the throat, armbar in a clinch, late punches, low blows, step on an opponent's foot and punch, continuous headbutting and making it look accidental.

Down for the Count

A boxer who is knocked down for the count of 10.

Draw

A draw is when both boxers tie or earn equal number of points from the judges scoring the fight. Example: 114-114, 114-114, 114-114

F

Feint

A feint is a fake punch or any offensive movement used to get your opponent to react and move out of his good offensive position, opening himself up to your real attack.

Fouls

Fouls are actions by a boxer that the referee doesn't feel meet the standard of a fair blow, or unsportsmanlike conduct. There are intentional fouls and accidental fouls. The most common fouls are headbutts, holding and low blows.

G

Gate

The gate is the total amount of money that a boxing match brings in from the people who attended it.

Glass Jaw

A boxer who is especially susceptible to a knockout is said to have a glass jaw or glass chin.

Go the Distance

A boxer goes the distance when he can fight through all the scheduled rounds.

Go to the Scorecards

Go to the scorecards means that after a fight has gone its scheduled number of rounds, the judges' score cards will determine the winner. It is also used when there is a fight stoppage due to an accidental head butt if the fight has gone beyond four rounds.

Granite Jaw*

A boxer who can take a punch to the head and keep fighting is said to have a granite jaw.

H

Haymaker

A haymaker is a wild swinging punch thrown with all of the person's weight behind it in an attempt to knock out the other person. You usually see haymakers in street fighting or in the movies. Haymakers are also used in boxing as a last resort. They deliver enough force to break a man's jaw.

The term first appeared in 1912, perhaps from the 1880 "hit the hay" or "go to sleep".

Headbutt

A headbutt occurs when a boxer's head is brought forward beyond his or her leading foot and gloves. The head is then swung left or right or up and down and it strikes the opponent. Headbutts can cause a serious cut or damaging head blow. It's up to the referee to determine whether a headbutt is accidental or intentional.

Hitting on the Break

Hitting on the break occurs when the referee breaks apart two boxers who are clinching and one boxer immediately hits his opponent instead of taking a mandatory full step back.

Hook

A hook is an inside power punch. It's a short sideways punch delivered with the elbow bent so the arm forms sort of a hook. The temple, side of the jaw, ribs and liver is the target.

I

Infighting

Fighting at close range.

J

Jab

The jab is the busiest punch in boxing. It's a punch thrown quickly with your leading hand straight from the chin in direct line to your target.

Journeyman

A journeyman is a boxer with good boxing skills who strives to succeed but who has limitations and little or no expectations of winning a fight. Journeymen are often hired on short notice to fight up-and-coming prospects and contenders to pad their records.

K

Kidney Punch

A kidney punch is a blow to the lower back which is illegal in boxing due to the damage it causes to one's kidneys.

Knockdown

A knockdown occurs when a boxer get hits and touches the floor with any part of his body other than his feet, is being held up by the ropes, or is hanging on, through, or over the ropes and cannot protect himself or fall to the floor.

Knockout (KO)

A boxer loses by way of knockout or KO when he or she is unable to get up unassisted after being floored by the count of 10.

L

Liver Punch

A liver punch is a short quick punch to the liver delivered with a left hook. It's one of the most devastating punches in boxing guaranteed to bring you right down. It's sickening as well as paralyzing.

M

Majority Decision (MD)

A majority decision occurs when two of the three judges score one boxer as the winner, while the third judge scores neither boxer a winner (a draw). Example: 116-114, 116-114, 114-114

Manager

A manager in boxing is a person who gets paid to act as the boxer's agent or representative. It's unlawful for a manager to have a direct or indirect financial interest in the promotion of a boxer or to get paid from a promoter except if it's in the manager's contract with the boxer. These rules only apply to fights of 10 rounds or more. A boxer can act as his or her own manager.

Mandatory Eight Count

A mandatory eight count is an 8 second count that a fallen boxer must take when he gets back on his feet. It allows the referee time to decide whether the boxer can continue the fight.

Marquess of Queensberry Rules

The Marquess of Queensberry Rules sponsored by British John Sholto Douglas, 9th Marquess of Queensberry in 1867 became the foundation of modern boxing regulations.

Matchmaker

A matchmaker in boxing is a person who proposes, selects, and arranges a fight between boxers.

Mouse

A swelling on the face, forehead or head.

N

Neutral Corner

One of two corners of a boxing ring that are not assigned to either boxer during a fight. There are no chairs or any members of a boxer's team in a neutral corner aka white corner. After a boxer has knocked down his opponent he is required to go to a neutral corner while the referee does the count.

No-Decision (ND)

If a fight is scheduled for more than four rounds and an accidental foul occurs causing an injury severe enough for the referee to stop the fight, then the fight will result in a No Decision or ND if stopped before four completed rounds. (Per ABC, IBF, WBA, WBO, Nevada Athletic Commission rules.)

O

Orthodox

Refers to a right-handed fighter.

On the Ropes

Refers to a boxer on the verge of defeat who has been knocked against the ropes and kept there by his or her opponent's blows.

Outside Fighter

An outside fighter or range fighter tries to maintain that gap between himself and his opponent, fighting with longer range punches. Outside fighters have to be fast on their feet, stepping in with a jab and stepping back out of range quickly to evade their opponent.

P

Palooka

A palooka is a tenth rater, a nobody, and a lousy boxer with no ability who usually loses his fights in four or six rounds to boxers who are just starting out in their careers. It's synonymous with tomato can or ham and egger. There was a comic strip created by Ham Fisher in 1928 that featured a good-hearted, slow-witted and inarticulate boxer named Joe Palooka.

Peek-a-Boo

In the Peek-a-Boo style, a boxer holds his hands high in front of his face. Floyd Patterson and Mike Tyson used the

Cus D' Amato forearms-up peek-a-boo. Archie Moore used the arms-across peek-a-boo.

Pitty-Pat Punches

Pitty-pat punches lack intensity when they connect. They're the kind of punches seen in amateur boxing that rack up points but have no destructive effect. Also referred to as cheap punches, pitty-patty punches or pitty-patty slaps.

Pound-for-Pound

Pound-for-Pound or P4P means the best boxer overall based upon his or her boxing skills whatever the weight. Pound-for-pound rankings compare boxers regardless of weight by using criteria such as boxing records, percentage of wins by knockout and level of competition to determine who is the better boxer.

Power Punches

Power punches are hooks, straight rights or lefts, uppercuts, or stiff jabs. Power punches are solid punches to the chin, head, or body that inflict damage.

Promoter

A promoter in boxing is the person primarily responsible for organizing, promoting, and putting on a professional boxing match. Usually it's not the hotel, casino or venue where the fight is going to be held unless they are the primary ones putting the fight on and there isn't a promoter. It's unlawful for a promoter to have any direct or indirect financial interest in the promotion of a boxer. These rules only apply to fights of 10 rounds or more. A boxer can act as his or her own promoter.

Pull One's Punches

A boxer is said to pull his or her punches when he or she uses less force than capable of, holds back from using all ones strength.

Punch

Basic punches in boxing are the jab, straight right (cross), uppercut and hook. Then you have the corkscrew delivered off a jab or cross and the wide swinging uppercut called the bolo punch.

Purse

The purse is money paid to two professional boxers for engaging in a fight. The amount of the purse is contractually guaranteed prior to the fight and is not altered by the outcome of the fight. Promoters pay the boxers the purse and out of the purse a boxer pays his cornermen (manager, trainer and cutman) a percentage. Sanctioning bodies also demand a percentage of the purse. Boxers usually end up with 50 to 70 percent before taxes.

R

Ring Generalship

Ring generalship applies to the fighter who uses skills beyond straight punching power to control the action in the ring.

Ring Magazine Belts

The Ring magazine issues belts to the top man of a division. The holder of the belt is considered the undisputed world champion of that division. *The Ring* Champions lose their belt and title only if they retire, move to another weight division or are defeated in a championship bout. Unlike the other alphabet boxing sanctioning bodies *The Ring* does not declare interim champions or strip champions of their belt. Vacancies can be filled by winning a fight between the number 1 and number 2 or under certain circumstances between the number 1 and number 3 contenders of a division. There are 10 contenders in each of the 17 divisions.

Rope-a-Dope

Rope-a-dope was used by Muhammad Ali in his 1974 fight against George Foreman. It involves lying back on the ropes, shelling up and allowing your opponent to throw punches until they tire themselves out and then you exploit their defensive flaws and nail them.

Rounds

Professional boxing matches cannot be scheduled for more than 12 rounds for males or 10 rounds for females. Each round lasts three minutes for males and two minutes for females with a one-minute rest between rounds.

Rubber Match

A rubber match is the deciding match in a series of fights between two boxers where each boxer has won a fight against the other. Rubber match usually refers to the third fight in a series, a trilogy. It's seen as the match that determines which boxer is really the best.

Rules of Boxing

Boxing rules can vary from country to country, state to state, by boxing organization, and whether the fight is amateur or professional. Most sanctioned fights today follow the Association of Boxing Commissions unified rules.

S

Sanctioning Body

Sanctioning bodies are boxing sanctioning organizations that sponsor championship fights and awards title belts. The World Boxing Association (WBA, the oldest), World Boxing Council (WBC), World Boxing Organization (WBO) and International Boxing Federation (IBF) are examples the major groups.

Saved by the Bell

Saved by the bell is when the bell rings signaling the end of the round before the referee finishes his count. This phrase came into being in the latter half of the nineteenth century.

Southpaw

Southpaws are left handed fighters (unorthodox). They put their right foot forward, jab with their right hand and throw power punches with their left hand (rear hand).

Split Decision (SD)

A split decision occurs when two of the three judges score one boxer as the winner, while the third judge scores the other boxer as the winner. Example: 116-114, 116-114, 113-115

Standing Eight Count

A standing eight count occurs when the referee stops the fight and counts to eight. During this time the referee will determine if the boxer can continue. In some amateur and professional fights, a knocked down boxer must take a mandatory eight count even if he or she has gotten up immediately.

Stick and Move

Stick and move is when a boxer jabs or uses long range punches then quickly steps backwards using elusive footwork to evade their opponent.

Straight Right

A straight right is considered a power punch. If you are a right handed boxer it's a straight right. If you are a left handed boxer it's a straight left.

Sucker Punch

An unexpected punch that catches a person completely off guard.

T

Take a Dive

To throw a fight. To intentionally pretend to get knocked out by a light punch, thus intentionally losing the fight. A fixed fight with an unlawful prearranged outcome.

Technical Knockout (TKO)

A boxer loses by technical knockout or TKO if the referee intercedes and stops the fight declaring them unable to continue because of bad cuts or bruises, they cannot go on, or cannot defend themselves.

Ten Point Must System

In the 10 Point Must System of scoring a fight, the winner of a round must receive 10 points. The loser of a round will receive from 9 to 6 points. A close round: 10-9. One knockdown: 10-8. Two knockdowns: 10-7. Three knockdowns: 10-6. No knockdown but one fighter completely dominates round: 10-8. Can't pick a winner: 10-10.

The Sweet Science

The Sweet Science is a collection of boxing articles written by A.J. Liebling that appeared in *The New Yorker* from 1951 through 1963. Liebling was a devotee of boxing writer, Pierce Egan who published *Boxiana*, a chronicle of bare-knuckle fighting in the early nineteenth century. Egan described boxing as "the sweet science" and "the sweet science of bruising". Liebling cited Egan frequently and named his collection *The Sweet Science* in honor of Egan.

Throw in the Towel

To throw in the towel also, to throw in the sponge is to end the fight, to give up, acknowledge defeat. When a boxer's second (his trainer or corner man) feels his boxer is taking a beating and doesn't think he can or should continue the fight he throws a towel or sponge into the ring to stop the carnage, to end the fight by TKO.

Tomato Can

A lousy fighter who usually loses in four or five rounds to boxers just starting out in their careers or to experienced boxers taking a bout just to stay in shape. Tomato Cans are known for bleeding, losing and taking a beating.

U

Unanimous Decision (UD)

A unanimous decision occurs when all three judges agree on a winner. Example: 116-114, 116-114, 115-113

Undisputed Champion*

In professional boxing, the undisputed champion of a weight class is a boxer who is recognized as the world champion at that class by all of the major sanctioning bodies. Which bodies are considered "major" varies, but the list would be expected to include the World Boxing Association (WBA), World Boxing Council (WBC), World Boxing Organization (WBO), and the International Boxing Federation (IBF).

Unifying the Title*

The process by which a fighter is recognized as having won the title in a particular weight class by all major sanctioning bodies, thereby becoming the undisputed champion in that weight class

Upper Cut

Upper cuts are thrown at close range. The jaw or the solar plexus is the target. It's an infighter's best weapon.

W

Weight Classes

The four sanctioning bodies recognize 17 weight classes or weight divisions for professional male boxers. The weight classes for female boxers have a separate schedule.

Weigh-In

The weigh-in is a pre-fight ceremony where boxers are weighed to make sure they are within the limits for their weight classes and contracted weight for the fight.

White Collar Boxers

White collar boxers are not registered amateurs or professional boxers. They box (basically spar with an opponent) in contests or exhibitions where no cash prizes are awarded, nor is a winner or a loser declared.

*All terms except those with an asterisk (*) are from Gus Petropulos, "Ringside by Gus," http://www.ringsidebygus.com/boxing-terms.html, accessed May 27, 2009.

Notes

Opening Quote

1. Page vi: " . . . and hardly merely a game." Oates, Joyce Carol. *On Boxing*. Originally published in 1987 by Dolphin/Doubleday. New York: First Ecco Edition, *An Imprint* of HarperCollins Publishers, 2002, page 18.

Introduction

1. Page xiv: ". . . or you lose." Oates, Joyce Carol. *On Boxing*. Originally published in 1987 by Dolphin/Doubleday. New York: First Ecco Edition, *An Imprint* of HarperCollins Publishers, 2002, page 138.
2. Page xiv: " . . . only one climbs out." Oates, Joyce Carol. *On Boxing*. Originally published in 1987 by Dolphin/Doubleday. New York: First Ecco Edition, *An Imprint* of HarperCollins Publishers, 2002, page 151.
3. Page xiv: " . . . But the fighter still remains." Paul Simon, "The Boxer." Edited by Robert Hedin and Michael Waters. *Perfect in Their Art—Poems on Boxing From Homer to Ali*. Carbondale: Southern Illinois University Press, 2003, page 171.

Round One:
Courage and Confidence—*Muhammad Ali*

1. Page 3: " . . . have the courage to go after." Hauser, Thomas, with the cooperation of Muhammad Ali. *Muhammad Ali, His Life and Times.* New York: Simon & Schuster Paperbacks, 1992, page 201.
2. Page 10: " . . . with them Viet Cong." "'The Greatest' Is Gone" (http://www.time.com/time/magazine/article/0,9171,919377-5,00.html). *Time.* February 27, 1978, p. 5. Retrieved on March 3, 2009.
3. Page 10: " . . . never called me nigger." "This Week in Black History" (http://findarticles.com/p/articles/mi_m1355/is_n26_v85/ai_15407999). *Jet.* May 2, 1994. Retrieved on March 3, 2009.
4. Page 14: " . . . that's a sissy punch."' Dundee, Angelo with Bert Randolph Sugar. *My View From The Corner.* New York: The McGraw-Hill Companies, 2008, page 187.

Round Two:
Great Opponents Make Great Champions—*Jack Dempsey and Gene Tunney*

1. Page 32: " . . . straighter hitter than Dempsey." Evans, Gavin. *Kings of the Ring, The History of Heavyweight Boxing.* London: Weidenfeld & Nicholson, The Orion Publishing Group, Ltd., 2005, page 85.
2. Page 32: " . . . that he tires quickly." Evans, Gavin. *Kings of the Ring, The History of Heavyweight Boxing.* London: Weidenfeld & Nicholson, The Orion Publishing Group, Ltd., 2005, page 85.
3. Page 36: ' . . . wonderful period of the past.' Evans, Gavin. *Kings of the Ring, The History of Heavyweight Boxing.* London: Weidenfeld & Nicholson, The Orion Publishing Group, Ltd., 2005, page 87.

Round Three:
Challenging Yourself—*Oscar De La Hoya*

1. Page 48: " . . . quarterback to run the show.'" De La Hoya, Oscar, with Steve Springer. *American Son.* New York: HarperColllins Publishers, 2008, page 182.

Round Four:
The Quality of Being Tough—*Jake LaMotta*

1. Page 53: " . . . anyone else ever saw." Mercante, Arthur. *Inside the Ropes.* Ithica, NY: McBooks Press, Inc., 2006, pages 56-57.
2. Page 54: " . . . I killed them or they killed me." Syed, Matthew. "The raging bull who refuses to give up fight with life." *TimesOnLine.* http:www.timesonline.co.uk/tol/sport/more_sport/article2434600,ece, September 11, 2007. Retrieved on January 11, 2009.
3. Page 55: " . . . A car." Mercante, Arthur. *Inside the Ropes.* Ithica, NY: McBooks Press, Inc., 2006, page 130.
4. Page 56: " . . . and slug and slug and slug." LaMotta, Jake, with Joseph Carter and Peter Savage. *Raging Bull.* Englewood Cliffs, NJ: First Da Capo Press, paperback edition, 1997, page 76. Originally published: Englewood Cliffs, N.J.: Prentice-Hall, 1970.
5. Page 60: " . . . 1977 75th Anniversary' awards." Thomas, Allyn. "The Jake LaMotta Story. (http://www.britishboxing.net/news_4093-The-Jake-La-Motta-Story.html). *BritishBoxing.net.* December 4, 2008. Retrieved on January 13, 2009.
6. Page 61: " . . . not afraid of none of them rats." Conway, Brett. "The Fix, LaMotta's Dive, and the Outfoxing of Fox.", (http://www.maxboxing.com/conway/conway101206.asp). *MaxBoxing LLC.* October 12, 2006. Retrieved on January 13, 2009.

Round Five:

Reinventing Oneself and Making a Comeback—*George Foreman*

1. Page 65: "... boxing—nay, all of sports." Sugar, Bert Randolph. *Boxing's Greatest Fighters.* Guilford, CT.: The Globe Pequot Press, 2006, page 98.
2. Page 66: "... Hits like Jack Dempsey."' Foreman, George and Joel Engel. *By George, The Autobiography of George Foreman.* New York: Villard Books, 1995, page 8.
3. Page 73: "... I proved the point."' Schulberg, Budd. *Sparring with Hemingway and Other Legends of the Fight Game.* Chicago: Ivan R. Dee, 1995, page 233.

Round Six:

Overcoming Obstacles/Persistence & Determination —*James J. Braddock*

1. Page 90: "... only thing in his life that did.'" Schaap, Jeremy. *Cinderella Man.* Boston: Houghton Mifflin Company, 2005, page 276.

Round Seven:

Winning Without Shortcuts—*Joe Calzaghe*

1. Page 95: "Crazy." Calzaghe, Joe. *No Ordinary Joe.* London: Century, The Random House Group Limited, 2007, pages 70.
2. Page 96: "... the feeling you need to have." Calzaghe, Joe. *No Ordinary Joe.* London: Century, The Random House Group Limited, 2007, page 68.
3. Page 96: "... Joe would never cheat." Calzaghe, Joe. *No Ordinary Joe.* London: Century, The Random House Group Limited, 2007, page 69.

4. Page 103: " . . . and I did it the hard way." Calzaghe, Joe. *No Ordinary Joe.* London: Century, The Random House Group Limited, 2007, page 68.

Round Eight:

Making Fear Your Friend—*Floyd Patterson*

1. Page 109: " . . . safety in the darkness for me." Patterson, Floyd, with Milton Gross. *Victory Over Myself.* New York: Bernard Geis Associates, distributed by Random House, 1962, page 9.
2. Page 110: " . . . be quicker and more alert." Hauser, Thomas. *The Black Lights.* New York: McGraw-Hill Book Company, 1986, page 20.
3. Page 111:" . . . against another fighter." Hauser, Thomas. *The Black Lights.* New York: McGraw-Hill Book Company, 1986, page 20.
4. Page 112: " . . . before his opponent could recover from the first." Arnold, Peter. *The Pictoral History of Boxing,* New York: Gallery Books, A Division of W.H. Smith Publishers Inc., 1988, page 121.
5. Page 115: " . . . I've grown out of that." Litsky, Frank. "Floyd Patterson, Boxing Champion, Dies at 71." (http://www.nytimes.com/2006/05/11sports/othersports/11cnd-patterson.html). *The New York Times.* May 11, 2006. Retrieved on December 5, 2008.
6. Page 116: " . . . also got up more than anyone." Goldman, Tom. "Former Heavyweight Champ Floyd Patterson Dies." (http://www.npr.org/templates/story/story.php?storyId=539849). *NPR.* Retrieved on July 7, 2009.

Round Nine:

Overcoming Pain—*Rocky Marciano*

1. Page 123: " . . . didn't do anything right."' Sugar, Bert Randolph. *Boxing's Greatest Fighters.* Guilford, CT.: The Globe Pequot Press, 2006, page 43.

2. Page 124: " . . . excluded from consciousness." Oates, Joyce Carol. *On Boxing.*Originally published in 1987 by Dolphin/Doubleday. New York: First Ecco Edition, *An Imprint* of HarperCollins Publishers, 2002, page 29.
3. Page 125: " . . . guy on earth I want to fight." Evans, Gavin. *Kings of the Ring, The History of Heavyweight Boxing.* London: Weidenfeld & Nicholson, The Orion Publishing Group, 2005, page 125.

Round Ten:

Discipline and Preparation—*Bernard Hopkins*

1. Page 136: ' . . . a gift few fighters have.'" Sugar, Bert Randolph. Boxing's Greatest Fighters. Guilford, CT.: The Globe Pequot Press, 2006, page 311.
2. Page 139: " . . . he takes care of himself." Rafael, Dan. "Hopkins can't stay out of the ring; now he wants Wright." http://sports.espn.go.com/sports/boxing/columns/story?columnist=rafael_dan&id=2943120). ESPN.com. July 20, 2007. (Retrieved on January 10, 2009.

Round Eleven:

Maintaining Dignity Through Victory and Defeat—*Joe Louis and and Max Schmeling*

1. Page 153: " . . . in the history of the world." Ross Greenberg and Rick Bernstein, Executive Producers; Joseph M. Lavine; Producer; Ouisie Shapiro, Writer. *Joe Louis, America's Hero . . . Betrayed.* An HBO Sports Presentation, 2008.
2. Page 153: " . . . too out of it to get involved." Schmeling, Max. *Max Schmeling: An Autobiography.* Translated and edited by George B. von der Lippe. Chicago: Bonus Books, 1998, page 155.

3. Page 157: " . . . he once said." Evans, Gavin. *Kings of the Ring, The History of Heavyweight Boxing.* London: Weidenfeld & Nicholson, The Orion Publishing Group, 2005, page 97.
4. Page 158: " . . . I loved him." Margolick, David. *Beyond Glory: Joe Louis vs. Max Schmeling, and a World on the Brink.* New York: Alfred A. Knopf, 2005, page 351. As quoted in the *Los Angeles Times*, December 28, 1988.

Round Twelve:
The Championship Round: Giving Back—*Wladimir and Vitali Klitschko*

1. Page 167: " . . . to hold it in the family." Evans, Gavin. *Kings of the Ring, The History of Heavyweight Boxing.* London: Weidenfeld & Nicholson, The Orion Publishing Group, 2005, page 221.

Selected Bibliography

Books

Arnold, Peter. *The Pictoral History of Boxing,* New York, New York: Gallery Books, A Division of W.H. Smith Publishers Inc., 1988.

Calzaghe, Joe, *No Ordinary Joe.* London: Century, The Random House Group Limited, 2007.

De La Hoya, Oscar, with Steve Springer. *American Son.* New York: HarperColllins Publishers, 2008.

Dundee, Angelo with Bert Randolph Sugar. *My View From The Corner.* New York: The McGraw-Hill Companies, 2008.

Foreman, George and Joel Engel. *By George, The Autobiography of George Foreman.* New York: Villard Books, 1995.

Evans, Gavin. *Kings of the Ring, The History of Heavyweight Boxing.* London: Weidenfeld & Nicholson, The Orion Publishing Group, Ltd., 2005.

Hauser, Thomas, with the cooperation of Muhammad Ali. *Muhammad Ali, His Life and Times.* New York: Simon & Schuster Paperbacks, 1992

Hauser, Thomas. *The Black Lights.* New York: McGraw-Hill Book Company, 1986.

Hedin, Robert and Michael Waters, editors. *Perfect in Their Art—Poems on Boxing From Homer to Ali.* Carbondale: Southern Illinois University Press, 2003.

LaMotta, Jake, with Joseph Carter and Peter Savage. *Raging Bull.* Englewood Cliffs, N.J.: First Da Capo Press, paperback edition,

1997, page 76. Originally published: Englewood Cliffs, N.J.: Prentice-Hall, 1970.

Margolick, David. *Beyond Glory: Joe Louis vs. Max Schmeling, and a World on the Brink.* New York: Alfred A. Knopf, 2005.

Mercante, Arthur. *Inside the Ropes.* Ithica, N.Y.: McBooks Press, Inc., 2006.

Oates, Joyce Carol. *On Boxing.* Originally published in 1987 by Dolphin/Doubleday. New York: First Ecco Edition, *An Imprint* of HarperCollins Publishers, 2002.

Patterson, Floyd, with Milton Gross. *Victory Over Myself.* New York: Bernard Geis Associates, distributed by Random House, 1962.

Schaap, Jeremy. *Cinderella Man.* Boston: Houghton Mifflin Company, 2005.

Schmeling, Max. *Max Schmeling: An Autobiography.* Translated and edited by George B. von der Lippe. Chicago: Bonus Books, 1998.

Schulberg, Budd. *Sparring with Hemingway and Other Legends of the Fight Game.* Chicago: Ivan R. Dee, 1995.

Sugar, Bert Randolph. *Boxing's Greatest Fighters.* Guilford, CT.: The Globe Pequot Press, 2006.

Publications and Newspaper Articles

Conway, Brett. "The Fix, LaMotta's Dive, and the Outfoxing of Fox." MaxBoxing LLC, http://www.maxboxing.com/conway/conway101206.asp, October 12, 2006, accessed January 13, 2009.

Goldman, Tom. "Former Heavyweight Champ Floyd Patterson Dies." NPR. http://www.npr.org/templates/story/story.php?storyId=539849, accessed July 7, 2009.

Jet. "This Week in Black History" (http://findarticles.com/p/articles/mi_m1355/is_n26_v85/ai_15407999). May 2, 1994, accessed March 3, 2009.

Litsky, Frank. "Floyd Patterson, Boxing Champion, Dies at 71." *The New York Times.* (http://www.nytimes.com/2006/05/11sports/othersports/11cnd-patterson.html), May 11, 2006, accessed December 5, 2008.

Petropulos, Gus. "Ringside by Gus," http://www.ringsidebygus.com/boxing-terms.html, accessed May 27, 2009.

Rafael, Dan. "Hopkins can't stay out of the ring; now he wants Wright." (http://sports.espn.go.com/sports/boxing/columns/story?columnist=rafael_dan&id=2943120, July 20, 2007. *ESPN.com,* accessed January 10, 2009.

Syed, Matthew. "The raging bull who refuses to give up fight with life." *TimesOnLine.* http:www.timesonline.co.uk/tol/sport/more_sport/article2434600,ece, September 11, 2007, accessed January 11, 2009.

Thomas, Allyn. "The Jake LaMotta Story." BritishBoxing.net, http://www.britishboxing.net/news_4093-The-Jake-La-Motta-Story.html, December 4, 2008, accessed January 13, 2009.

Time. "The Greatest' Is Gone." (http://www.time.com/time/magazine/article/0,9171,919377-5,00.html). February 27, 1978, p. 5. Accessed March 3, 2009.

Film

Ross Greenberg and Rick Bernstein, Executive Producers; Joseph M. Lavine; Producer; Ouisie Shapiro, Writer. *Joe Louis, America's Hero . . . Betrayed.* An HBO Sports Presentation, 2008.

Index

Words of Gratitude

To those who have contributed so much (and many more too numerous to mention):

Irbin Gary Oden—my father, who introduced me to boxing and encouraged me to try it

Andrew Flach and June Eding—my publisher and editor, for their ideas, hard work and inspiration

Brooke L. Adams—for her incredible artistic talent which is showcased in the drawings in this book

Steve Lippman—for his advice on everything in this book

Bruce Silverglade—for his technical advice on this book, his constant efforts to improve the sport of boxing and his vision to create white collar boxing out of Gleason's Gym

Chris Angle—my regular sparring partner at the New York Athletic Club, who keeps me fit and ready

Richard Rubenstein, Dara Busch and Joel Masmanian—public relations professionals extraordinaire who have given this book a real head start

Emanuel Steward—for being in my corner in London for Hedge Fund Fight Night in 2004, his continuing work with the Kronk Gym Foundation, and all he does for the sport

Jack Kendrick—for his boxing coaching, inspirational poetry and constant encouragement

Tom Hexner, Len Hersh, Luke Davis, Jacqueline Zaslavsky, Noriel Flores, Payal Srinivasan and a host of others—for steadfast support at my "day job"

John Turco—for our three great fights, and for his courage to make a comeback after being gunned down on the streets of New York City

Terry McGhee–dedicated New York Athletic Club boxing coach, for his tenacity to make a comeback after crushing his spine and vertebrae in a swimming accident

Tom Hauser—my writing mentor and world class author

Bert Sugar—for his unparalleled knowledge of the history of the sport, his constant support of my writing and speaking activities, and being a part of this book